my Book Grade 4

Modules 6–10

Authors and Advisors

Alma Flor Ada • Kylene Beers • F. Isabel Campoy

Joyce Armstrong Carroll • Nathan Clemens

Anne Cunningham • Martha C. Hougen • Tyrone C. Howard

Elena Izquierdo • Carol Jago • Erik Palmer

Robert E. Probst • Shane Templeton • Julie Washington

Contributing Consultants

David Dockterman • Jill Eggleton

Printed in the U.S.A.

ISBN   978-0-358-46156-2

6 7 8 9 10 11 12 13   0029   30 29 28 27 26 25 24 23 22

4500852037

r1.21

Welcome to myBook!

Do you like to read different kinds of texts for all kinds of reasons? Do you have a favorite genre or author? What can you learn from a video? Do you think carefully about what you read and view?

Here are some tips to get the MOST out of what you read and view:

Set a Purpose. What is the title? What is the genre? What do you want to learn from this text or video? What about it looks interesting to you?

Read and Annotate. As you read, underline and highlight important words and ideas. Make notes about things you want to figure out or remember. What questions do you have? What are your favorite parts? Write them down!

Make Connections. How does the text or video connect to what you already know? To other texts or videos? To your own life or community? Talk to others about your ideas. Listen to their ideas, too.

Wrap It Up! Look back at your questions and annotations. What did you like best? What did you learn? What do you still want to know? How will you find out?

As you read the texts and watch the videos in this book, make sure you get the MOST out of them by using the tips above.

But, don't stop there . . . Decide what makes you curious, find out more about it, have fun, and never stop learning!

MODULE 6

Marvels of Nature

🌱 **SCIENCE CONNECTION:** Natural Wonders **10**

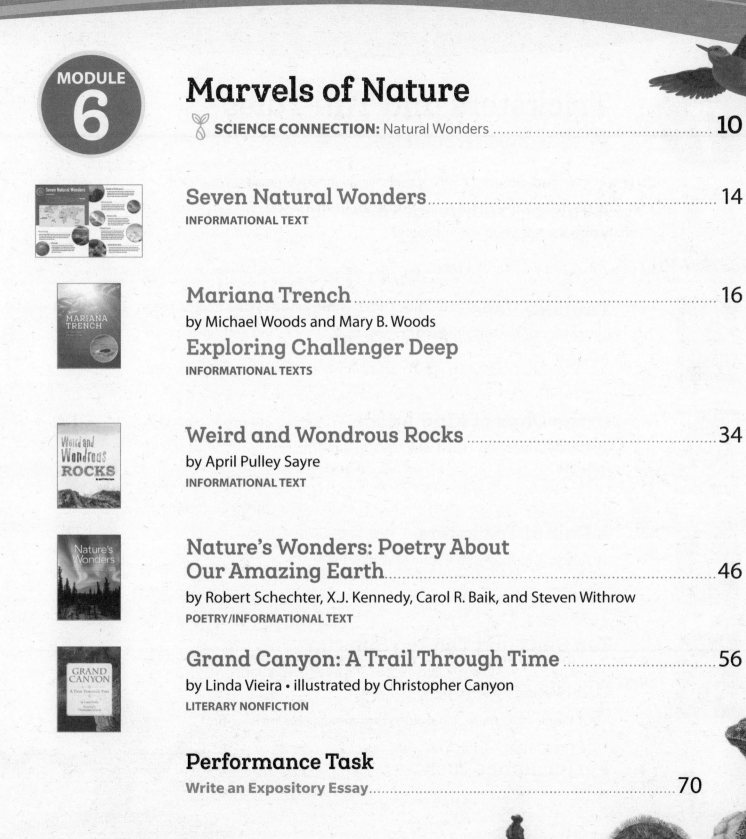

Seven Natural Wonders **14**
INFORMATIONAL TEXT

Mariana Trench **16**
by Michael Woods and Mary B. Woods
Exploring Challenger Deep
INFORMATIONAL TEXTS

Weird and Wondrous Rocks **34**
by April Pulley Sayre
INFORMATIONAL TEXT

**Nature's Wonders: Poetry About
Our Amazing Earth** **46**
by Robert Schechter, X.J. Kennedy, Carol R. Baik, and Steven Withrow
POETRY/INFORMATIONAL TEXT

Grand Canyon: A Trail Through Time **56**
by Linda Vieira • illustrated by Christopher Canyon
LITERARY NONFICTION

Performance Task
Write an Expository Essay **70**

MODULE 7

Tricksters and Tall Tales

🌐 **SOCIAL STUDIES CONNECTION:** Traditional Tales **74**

A Tale of Traditional Tales 78
INFORMATIONAL TEXT

Thunder Rose 80
by Jerdine Nolen • illustrated by Kadir Nelson
TALL TALE

In the Days of King Adobe 100
as told by Joe Hayes • illustrated by Ute Simon
FOLKTALE

A Pair of Tricksters 112
by Aesop and John and Caitlín Matthews •
illustrated by Maribel Lechuga and Jui Ishida
FABLE/TRICKSTER TALE

Ten Suns and The Ten Suns 122
retold by Eric A. Kimmel • illustrated by Yongsheng Xuan;
video directed by Oded Levy
LEGEND and VIDEO

Performance Task
Write an Expository Essay 142

MODULE 8

Food for Thought

 SCIENCE CONNECTION: Food and Nutrition..................................... **146**

To Your Health! 150
INFORMATIONAL TEXT

Eco-Friendly Food 152
by Cath Senker
INFORMATIONAL TEXT

Kids Rock Nutrition in the Kitchen 164
from Nutrition.gov
COOKING VIDEO

Bug Bites 170
INFORMATIONAL TEXT

Now You're Cooking! 180
by René Saldaña, Jr. • illustrated by Jonathan Allardyce
REALISTIC FICTION/RECIPE

Performance Task
Write an Opinion Essay 194

MODULE 9

Global Guardians

❧ **SCIENCE CONNECTION:** Conservation **198**

The Eco Guardians 202
LETTERS

Luz Sees the Light 204
by Claudia Dávila
GRAPHIC NOVEL

On Sea Turtle Patrol and Saving the Kemp's Ridley Sea Turtle 238
by Nancy Dawson • illustrated by Denise Ortakales; video from Texas Parks and Wildlife
REALISTIC FICTION and INFORMATIONAL VIDEO

How Can We Reduce Household Waste? 252
by Mary K. Pratt
INFORMATIONAL/ARGUMENTATIVE TEXT

Seeds of Change 272
by Jen Cullerton Johnson • illustrated by Sonia Lynn Sadler
BIOGRAPHY

Performance Task
Write an Opinion Essay 292

MODULE 10

Communication Nation

SOCIAL STUDIES CONNECTION: Communication **296**

How Technology Has Changed Communication 300
TIMELINE

The History of Communication 302
with illustrations by Danny Schlitz
INFORMATIONAL TEXT

A New Language—Invented by Kids! 322
by Charnan Simon
NARRATIVE NONFICTION

Dolphin Dinner 330
from National Geographic Kids
INFORMATIONAL VIDEO

Cooper's Lesson 336
by Sun Yung Shin • illustrated by Kim Cogan
REALISTIC FICTION

Performance Task
Write an Expository Essay 354
Glossary 358

Marvels of Nature

"The wilderness holds answers to more questions than we yet know how to ask."

—Nancy Newhall

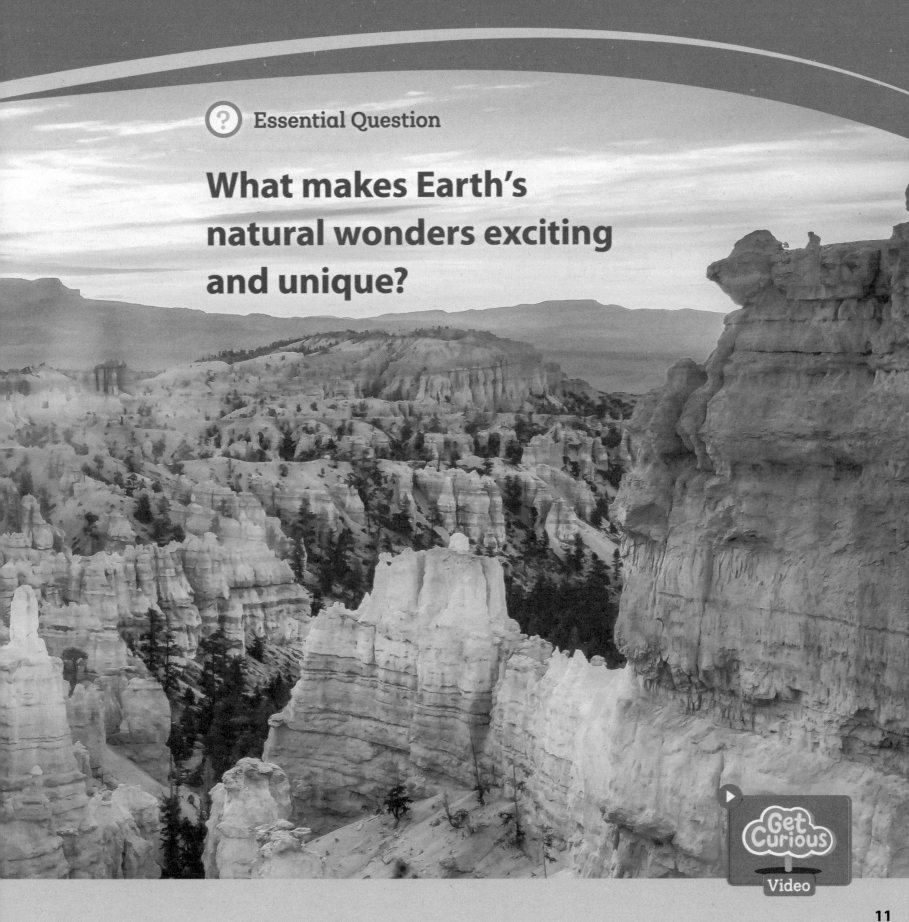

What makes Earth's natural wonders exciting and unique?

Get Curious

Video

Land

Natural
Wonders

Sky

Water

landform A landform is a natural feature, such as a mountain, of a land's surface.

canyon A canyon is a deep valley that has steep sides.

landscape When you look at a landscape, you are looking at the area of land around you.

scenic Something that is scenic has beautiful scenery.

 myNotes

Seven Natural Wonders

wonder

n. something extraordinary—a marvel

1 The world is full of wonders—unusual places with amazing landforms. Seven of these natural wonders are unique. They are known as the Seven Natural Wonders of the World.

Canada

USA

Mexico and Central America

South America

Europe

Africa

Asia

Australia

New Zealand

●Grand Canyon

2 Arizona's Grand Canyon is more than a mile deep and 200 miles long. The canyon offers spectacular natural views. But its colorful layers of rock aren't just breathtaking to look at; the layers give geologists valuable clues to our planet's past.

● Paricutín

3 This natural wonder literally rose from the earth as people watched. In 1943, a Mexican farmer marveled as the landscape of his farm changed before his eyes. A volcano grew from his cornfield. It reached 1,000 feet in just 10 months!

Harbor of Rio de Janeiro

4 The Harbor of Rio de Janeiro in Brazil is the world's largest deep-water bay. Majestic mountains fringe the shoreline, providing scenic views. The vertical contrast of towering peaks to golden beaches to deep valleys below is quite dramatic.

Aurora Borealis

5 The Aurora Borealis, or Northern Lights, illuminates the night sky above the North Pole with a natural light show. Charged particles collide with gases in Earth's atmosphere to create the colorful spectacle.

Victoria Falls

6 Victoria Falls in Zambia, Africa, is one of the world's largest waterfalls, stretching over 5,000 feet wide. A thick mist billows over 1,300 feet above the falls. The mist gave the falls its original name, "The Smoke That Thunders."

Mount Everest

7 The peak of Mount Everest is the highest point on the planet. Tectonic activity created the mountain long ago, when two huge plates deep within Earth's crust crashed together. The collision pushed the land above the plates higher and higher. Today only the bravest adventurers dare to climb to the top of the world.

Great Barrier Reef

8 The Great Barrier Reef stretches more than 1,000 miles across the waters off of the Australian coast. The skeletons of tiny sea creatures called *coral polyps* form the reef. The reef is one of the few living things on Earth visible from outer space.

Prepare to Read

GENRE STUDY **Informational texts** give facts and examples about a topic.

- An author's purpose for writing informational texts is to share facts about a topic.

- Authors of informational texts often organize their ideas using headings and subheadings.

- Informational texts include text and graphic features, such as captions, pronunciation guides, maps, and photographs.

SET A PURPOSE **Think about** the title and genre of this text. What do you want to learn about the Mariana Trench? Write your ideas below.

Build Background:
Coral Reefs

CRITICAL VOCABULARY

trench

summit

thrive

prehistoric

vital

glimpse

submersible

remotely

autonomous

MARIANA TRENCH

by Michael Woods
& Mary B. Woods

myNotes

CHINA

JAPAN

MARIANA ISLANDS

PHILIPPINES

MARIANA TRENCH

AUSTRALIA

NEW ZEALAND

PACIFIC OCEAN

1   Many people know that the highest point on Earth is at the top of Mount Everest. That famous peak towers 29,035 feet (8,850 m) above sea level. It is in the Himalaya Mountains, near the border of China and Nepal. But how many people can name the lowest place in the world? That point is at the bottom of the Mariana Trench, a valley in the floor of the Pacific Ocean. The trench lies just east of the Mariana Islands, southeast of China and Japan.

trench   A trench is a long, narrow groove or ditch.

This satellite photo of the Pacific Ocean shows the Mariana Trench as a dark blue crescent.

2   This enormous trench extends for about 1,554 miles (2,500 kilometers) from one end to the other. It could stretch from New York City almost to Denver, Colorado. The trench averages about 45 miles (72 km) wide. A person walking at a brisk pace would need about ten hours to go from one side to the other.

3   Inside that groove in the ocean floor is the Challenger Deep, the deepest spot in the world. It lies 210 miles (338 km) from the island of Guam. It is about 36,000 feet (11,000 m) below sea level—almost 7 miles (11 km) deep. If Mount Everest were placed in the Challenger Deep, the mountain's peak would still be under 7,000 feet (2,134 m) of water.

In this satellite image, the deepest areas of the Mariana Trench appear in dark blue.

Mount Everest, the highest point on Earth, lies on the border between Nepal and Tibet.

Flashlight fish have glowing patches just beneath their eyes.

WEIRD CREATURES

4 Conditions are very harsh at the **summit** of Mount Everest. Temperatures average –33°F (–36°C), and winter winds howl at more than 100 miles (161 km) an hour. Yet climbers have reached the top and lived to tell about it.

5 But no human, not even an expert diver, could survive the environment of the Challenger Deep. In this pitch-black world, the temperature is about 36°F (2°C). The human body shuts down quickly in water that cold. A person on the ocean floor also would be crushed by the weight of the water. Water is heavy. A 1-gallon (4-liter) milk jug holds about 8 pounds (3.6 kilograms) of water. At the deepest point in the ocean, water would press down with a weight heavier than hundreds of elephants.

> **summit**   The summit of a mountain is its top or highest point.

Ever Wonder?

6 Why is it pitch dark in the deep ocean? In the oceans, deeper means dimmer. Water absorbs and scatters sunlight. So, little light remains after 660 feet (201 m). Beyond that depth is a twilight zone, where the human eye cannot see colors. This zone of faint light goes down to about 3,300 feet (1,006 m). The midnight zone, from there on down, is in total darkness.

An anglerfish uses its natural fishing pole to lure prey into its mouth.

7   However, living things do **thrive** in the Mariana Trench. Some creatures look like deep-sea movie monsters or survivors from **prehistoric** times. These animals and plants are specially built for life in an extreme environment. Some can produce a glowing light, like fireflies. This is called bioluminescence. Creatures use this light to attract prey.

8   Anglerfish have bioluminescent, built-in fishing poles. In some of these fish, the pole is like an antenna growing from the top of the head. This rod glows in the dark water. The anglerfish waves it to attract other fish. When a fish approaches, the angler snaps up the prey in its huge mouth packed with long, needle-sharp teeth.

9   Flashlight fish also live in the Mariana Trench. Like the anglerfish, they are bioluminescent. The flashlight fish lurks in the dark water and turns its light on and off. When a curious fish approaches, it becomes dinner!

10   Certain types of crabs and bacteria thrive in the Mariana Trench. Scientists had never seen some of these until fairly recent deep-sea explorations. This is because the creatures can't exist anywhere else. The extreme temperatures and pressure of the deep ocean are **vital** to these organisms.

> ## "A world as strange as that of Mars."
>
> —William Beebe, an explorer, describing the deep ocean after setting a world record in 1934 by diving to 3,028 feet (923 m) in a submersible (small submarine)

---

thrive   When living things thrive, they grow well and are healthy.
prehistoric   Something that is prehistoric is very old, from a time before history was recorded.
vital   If something is vital, it is needed or very important.

CHALLENGER LOOKS DEEP

11   The Mariana Trench was discovered in 1875. Scientists on the British ship HMS *Challenger* used a machine to measure the ocean depth in different places. The machine unreeled a spool of wire with a heavy weight at the end. Dials measured the length of wire let out. When the weight touched bottom, scientists could tell the depth of the ocean floor. With that simple method, they realized that the water near the Mariana Islands was extremely deep.

12   In 1951 the British Royal Navy vessel HMS *Challenger II* returned to the area with a modern measuring device. It is called echo sounding, or sonar. It sends out sound waves that bounce off a surface, such as the seafloor. Scientists measured the time needed for sound waves to bounce back from the seafloor to the ship. This told them the ocean depth. Using echo sounding, *Challenger II* mapped the entire Mariana Trench. The deepest point it found was 35,760 feet (10,900 m). That point was named the Challenger Deep, after the ship.

The Moon over Mariana

13   Twelve U.S. astronauts have been on the moon. They explored the moon's surface in the 1960s and 1970s during the Apollo space program. However, only two people have ever visited the deepest place on Earth. Don Walsh (bottom, right) and Jacques Piccard (top, right) spent just twenty minutes there during their descent in the *Trieste* submersible in 1960.

A deep-sea submersible collects samples from the bottom of the Mariana Trench using a robotic arm.

14   People got their first **glimpse** of the Challenger Deep in 1960. That year scientist Jacques Piccard and U.S. Navy Lieutenant Don Walsh traveled to the bottom. They rode in the *Trieste* (TREE•est), a **submersible** vehicle. Small submarines of this kind are built to withstand extreme underwater pressure. They usually carry scientific instruments for exploring the deep ocean. Piccard and Walsh found a point deeper than *Challenger II* had found. It was 35,813 feet (10,916 m) below the surface. They also observed small fish near the ocean floor.

15   Since then oceanographers have used other vehicles and instruments to explore the deep ocean. Some are **remotely** operated vehicles, or ROVs. Scientists control these through cables from a ship on the surface. Others are **autonomous** underwater vehicles, or AUVs. These explore on their own without any connection to another ship. AUVs navigate with onboard computers and record data from the areas they explore.

16   In the 1990s, several Japanese ROVs explored the Mariana Trench. They observed shrimp, sandworms, and other living things. The ROV *Kaiko* scooped up samples of mud from the trench floor for scientists to study. Scientists found tiny organisms in those samples that are Earth's deepest living creatures.

glimpse   A glimpse is a very quick look at something.
submersible   If something is submersible, it can go or work under water.
remotely   If you use something remotely, you control it from a distance.
autonomous   If something is autonomous, it controls itself.

PLATES SO DEEP

17 The Mariana Trench is so deep because of movement in Earth's surface. Many huge plates of rock make up the surface. Earth's crust, or outer layer, forms the top of each plate. The bottom of each plate is part of Earth's mantle, the thick layer below the crust. The plates float on a layer of puttylike rock in the mantle. While floating, the edges of these plates slide past one another and bump into one another.

18 At the Mariana Trench, a heavy plate of rock on the ocean floor is pressing against a plate of lighter rock. When this happens, the heavier ocean plate plunges downward at a steep angle into Earth's mantle. The bottom of the Mariana Trench is where that heavy plate of rock is moving down into the mantle.

> ## "It's like a magic mirror."
> —Andy Rechnitzer, an oceanographer who planned the first dive into the Mariana Trench in 1960, describing the foreign world of the deep ocean

19 Plate movements have formed more than twenty other deep ocean trenches in different parts of the world. The Puerto Rico Trench, for instance, is the deepest place in the Atlantic Ocean. It lies north of the island of Puerto Rico. The trench is about 5 miles (8 km) deep and 1,100 miles (1,770 km) long.

Mariana Trench Expressway

20 Navy submarines patrolling the world's oceans like to stay in deep water. It is more difficult for enemies to detect them there. That's why U.S., Russian, and other submarines often use the Mariana Trench as an expressway. The trench is the main north-south route for submarines in the Pacific Ocean.

At the Mariana Trench, the movement of ocean plates into Earth's mantle created many underwater volcanoes. This cliff near the Mariana Trench shows layers of light and dark ash that collected on the seafloor during eruptions.

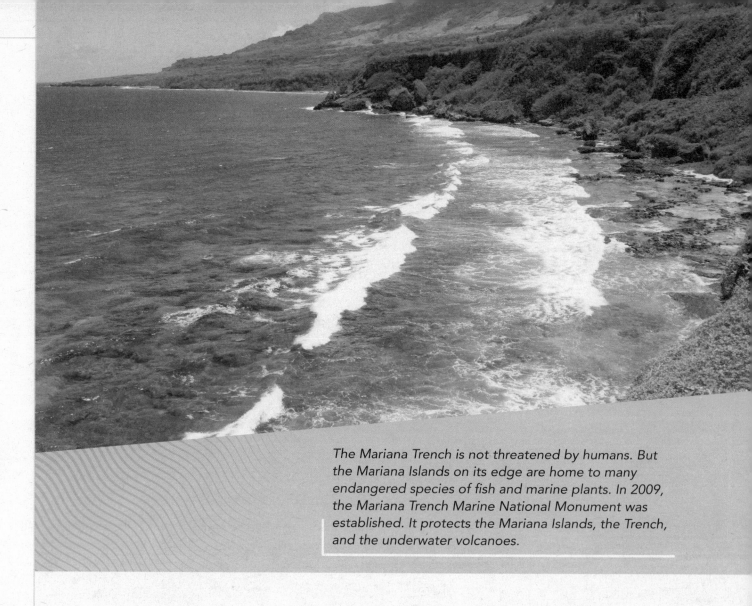

The Mariana Trench is not threatened by humans. But the Mariana Islands on its edge are home to many endangered species of fish and marine plants. In 2009, the Mariana Trench Marine National Monument was established. It protects the Mariana Islands, the Trench, and the underwater volcanoes.

WORRIES ABOUT THE WONDER

21 The future of the Mariana Trench seems very safe. Neither people nor nature threatens its existence. Ships sailing over the area do not cause any damage to the trench. However, movements of Earth's plates may eventually change the Mariana Trench. In millions of years, it may be deeper or shallower. But it is sure to remain a wonder that holds many secrets of the deep.

Exploring
CHALLENGER DEEP

1   After the Challenger Deep was discovered in 1875, explorers were anxious to visit this deepest point in the ocean. On January 23, 1960, an American submarine naval officer, Don Walsh, and a Swiss scientist, Jacques Piccard, traveled there in the U.S. Navy bathyscaphe [**băth'**•ə•skăf'] named *Trieste* [trē•**est'**]. This undersea research vehicle had five-inch-thick steel walls that would not crack under the extreme pressure so far below the ocean's surface.

2   In *Trieste's* very cramped space, Walsh and Piccard spent five hours descending 35,814 feet. At the bottom, they relayed their depth to their team. They were seven miles down! The bright headlight on their vehicle allowed them to see a foot-long flatfish and shrimp outside the porthole. Until then, no one had known that life existed in the Challenger Deep. After less than thirty minutes, the men unloaded the ballast and floated upward. More than three hours later, they reached the surface.

◄ *Trieste* was designed by Piccard's father with assistance from Jacques. *Trieste* can be seen at the National Museum of the U.S. Navy in Washington, D.C.

3   After this exploration, there were only two unmanned submarines that visited the Challenger Deep until March 25, 2012. That was when filmmaker James Cameron reached the bottom in the *Deepsea Challenger*. It took his tiny vehicle two hours and thirty-six minutes to make the descent. He was able to explore the sea floor for a few hours. He took video and collected samples from the ocean floor.

4   In May 2019, businessman Victor Vescovo reached the bottom of the Challenger Deep in a submarine called *DSV Limiting Factor*. During four hours on the seabed, Vescovo collected samples and may have discovered four new species. Onboard his support ship was Don Walsh, back for another look at this marvel of nature.

▲ Walsh is congratulated at the fiftieth anniversary of the *Trieste* exploration. Since his retirement from the Navy in 1975, he has continued exploring. He has participated in twenty-four submersible expeditions. He has also made more than seventy expeditions to the Arctic and the Antarctic. Walsh Spur, a pointed rock formation in Antarctica, is named for him.

Scuba divers:
130 feet

Deepest scuba dive ever:
1,082 feet

Deepest commercial dive:
1,752 feet

Navy submarines can operate at about 2,000 feet

Deepest recorded whale dive:
9,816 feet
(Cuvier's beaked whale)

Deepest fish found:
26,135 feet
(snailfish)

Challenger Deep bottom:
36,037 feet

Collaborative Discussion

Look back at what you wrote on page 16. Tell a partner two things you learned from this text. Then work with a group to discuss the questions below. Refer to details and examples in *Mariana Trench* and *Exploring Challenger Deep* to explain your answers. As your group works together, think carefully about each question.

1 Review page 20. What comparisons do the authors use to explain the size and depth of the Mariana Trench?

2 Reread pages 24–25 and pages 29–30. How are these two secondhand accounts alike? How are they different?

3 What are some of the ways that scientists have explored the trench? Why is it difficult to do research there?

Listening Tip

To be sure you understand, restate in your own mind what a speaker has said. Then ask yourself, "Do I agree with that idea? Is there something else I can add?"

Speaking Tip

Think about what you will say before you speak. Point out the text evidence you used to answer the questions.

Write a Response

PROMPT ···

Respond to the Text In *Mariana Trench* and *Exploring Challenger Deep,* you learned about the lowest place in the world. How would you describe the Mariana Trench? What makes it a unique natural wonder? Cite evidence from the text to support your response. Use some of the Critical Vocabulary words and some science words in your writing.

EVIDENCE ···

List details in *Mariana Trench* that describe the unique characteristics of this natural wonder.

Now write your response in a paragraph.

✓ Make sure your response

☐	uses evidence from the text to answer the questions.
☐	describes the Mariana Trench.
☐	explains what makes the Mariana Trench a unique natural wonder.
☐	includes Critical Vocabulary words and science words.
☐	is written in complete sentences.

Notice & Note
Contrasts and Contradictions

Prepare to Read

GENRE STUDY **Informational texts** give facts and examples about a topic.

- Authors may organize their ideas using headings. Headings and subheadings tell readers what the next section of text will be about.

- Authors of informational texts may organize their ideas by explaining causes and effects.

- Science texts also include words that are specific to the topic. These are words that name things or ideas.

SET A PURPOSE **Think about** rocks you see every day. Then look at the title and the photo on the next page. What types of rocks do you think you will read about? What do you want to learn about these rocks? Write your ideas below.

Meet the Author:
April Pulley Sayre

CRITICAL VOCABULARY

eternal

organic

intriguing

Weird and Wondrous ROCKS

by April Pulley Sayre

1   Call them natural wonders. Call them really weird rocks. In many of the United States' natural areas, rocks, not animals or plants, are the main attraction. There are musical rocks in Pennsylvania. There are rocks that put on a fire show in New York, and in Texas, rocks are the stars of an amazing art display. That's right! Rocks aren't just "sitting still" as you might expect. Now and then, rocks actually move across Death Valley's very flat floor. Read on to learn more about these weird and wondrous rocks!

Ringing Rocks County Park, Pennsylvania

2 A huge field in eastern Pennsylvania is full of mysterious rocks. When hit with a hammer, these rocks ring like bells. At Ringing Rocks County Park, visitors enjoy tapping the boulders to hear the sounds they make. Several musicians have even included the rocks' strange sounds in concerts!

3   The ringing rocks are made of diabase, a dark, igneous, or volcanic, rock. People used to think that not all of the rocks rang, but scientists have shown that they do. Some of the rocks produce sounds too low for humans to hear.

4   Some scientists think that high levels of iron in the rocks produce the ringing. Another theory points to stress caused by repeated freezing and thawing. The rocks and their sounds still need more study. In the meantime, the musical rocks provide great entertainment.

Eternal Flame Falls, New York

5 In Chestnut Ridge Park in western New York, a small
fire burns in a grotto, or hollow area, beneath . . . a
waterfall? The flame may have been burning, on and off, for
a thousand years. Hikers are told to carry barbecue lighters in
case the fire goes out. They may need to relight it,
because sometimes the flame needs help to be "eternal."

6   The Eternal Flame burns natural gas. The gas forms from decaying
organic matter and seeps out from shale rocks. Shale is a type of
sedimentary rock that contains fossilized organic matter—the remains
of ancient plants. The natural gas produces a flame up to 8 inches (20
cm) tall. The grotto protects the flame from wind and water.

7   Long-lasting flames burn in other places, too. Many are linked to
mines or volcanoes. Where natural gas burns, it usually forms from
super-hot underground shale. Still, a flame burning under a massive
waterfall makes Eternal Flame Falls truly unique and wondrous!

eternal	If something is eternal, it has no end and lasts forever.
organic	If something is organic, it is made up of living matter.

Caverns of Sonora, Texas

8 At first you might think you are on another planet. What surrounds you can't possibly be on Earth! The Caverns of Sonora is a seven-mile-long system of beautiful caves that lie beneath a Texas ranch. Legend says that a dog found the entrance to the caverns around 1900. In 1955, cavers crossed a ledge above a deep pit. They found passages leading to strange shapes and sparkling with crystals.

9 The caverns were formed by slow-moving water under the ground. The water dissolved the limestone layer and carried it away, forming the caverns. Water trickling through the cave walls over thousands of years has created some pretty amazing rock formations.

10 The water contains dissolved minerals. Drip by drip, as the water falls from the cave ceilings and walls, the minerals build up to form stalagmites and stalactites. Stalagmites grow up from cave floors. Stalactites grow downward from ceilings like icicles. Helictites are stalactites that grow in branching shapes. They can resemble teeth, drinking straws, or wings. Some of the deposits on the cave walls look like coral or popcorn. It can take centuries for these cave deposits to form, and the process continues today!

Helictites growing on cave wall ▶

Sailing Stones, Death Valley National Park, California

11   In Death Valley National Park, rocks seem to move on their own. They leave parallel tracks in the thick, deep mud of a remote playa, a dry lakebed. The rocks, which vary in weight from a few ounces to hundreds of pounds, can stand still for years at a time. Then, suddenly, hundreds of pebbles and boulders drift across the playa all at once. The only problem was that no one had ever seen this happen—they had only seen the puzzling tracks. Until recently, even scientists didn't know how the rocks moved!

12   To unlock this mystery, scientists set up a weather station to measure wind speed and rainfall. They installed tracking devices in rocks in a range of sizes up to about 36 pounds. They left time-lapse cameras in place to record movement.

13   Over time, rain and snow created a temporary pond a few inches deep. A thin layer of ice formed on top, trapping the rocks. Sunlight melted the ice enough to break it into large floating sheets. Then a mild wind pushed the ice sheets, which slowly dragged the rocks, leaving the telltale tracks. Mystery solved!

myNotes

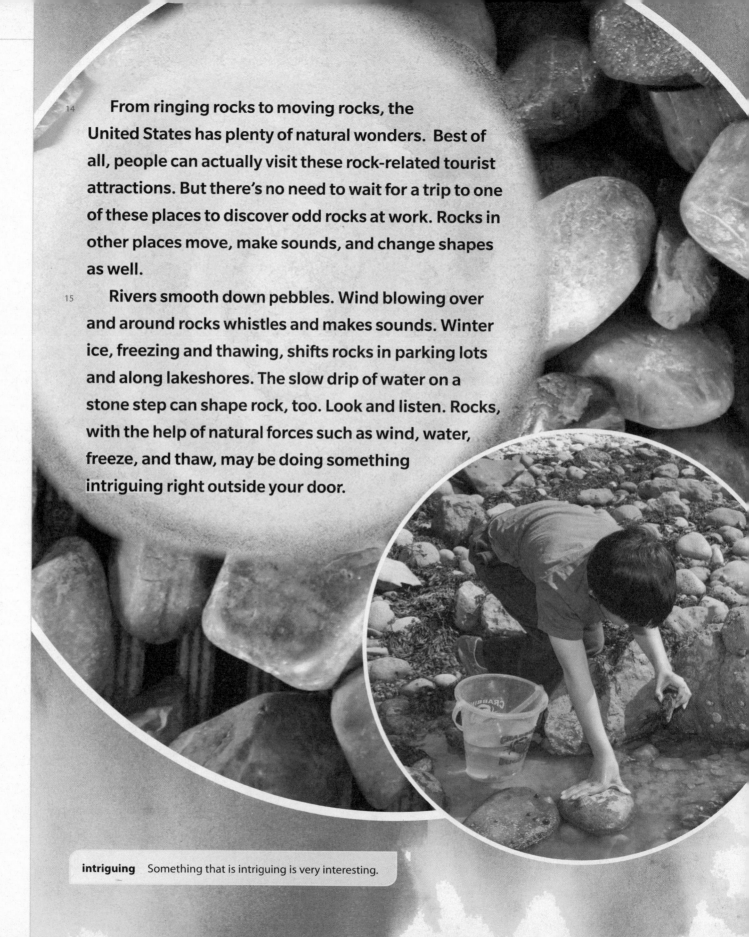

14   From ringing rocks to moving rocks, the United States has plenty of natural wonders. Best of all, people can actually visit these rock-related tourist attractions. But there's no need to wait for a trip to one of these places to discover odd rocks at work. Rocks in other places move, make sounds, and change shapes as well.

15   Rivers smooth down pebbles. Wind blowing over and around rocks whistles and makes sounds. Winter ice, freezing and thawing, shifts rocks in parking lots and along lakeshores. The slow drip of water on a stone step can shape rock, too. Look and listen. Rocks, with the help of natural forces such as wind, water, freeze, and thaw, may be doing something intriguing right outside your door.

intriguing   Something that is intriguing is very interesting.

Collaborative Discussion

Look back at what you wrote on page 34. Tell a partner what you learned in this text. Look for details in *Weird and Wondrous Rocks* to support your ideas as you make notes on the questions below. Then discuss the questions with a group. Keep the discussion moving forward by linking each new idea to what has been said.

1 Reread page 37. What details help you understand how the rocks were formed?

Listening Tip

As you listen to each speaker's ideas, think about how your own ideas connect to or build on them.

2 Reread page 38. Why do the flames need help to be "eternal" sometimes? Why is the word *eternal* in quotation marks?

Speaking Tip

Before you speak, point out how your comment will connect to or build on what another speaker has said. Cite evidence in the text that supports your comment.

3 Review page 39. What comparisons does the author use to help you picture the stalactites and other rock formations?

Write a Response

PROMPT

Respond to the Text In *Weird and Wondrous Rocks,* you learned about unusual rocks in the United States and what makes them weird and wondrous. How would you describe these natural wonders? What makes them weird and wondrous? Cite evidence from the text to support your response.

EVIDENCE

List details in *Weird and Wondrous Rocks* that tell what makes these natural wonders unique.

WRITE

Now write your response in a paragraph.

Make sure your response

☐ answers the questions.

☐ describes the different types of rocks in the selection.

☐ explains what makes the rocks weird and wondrous.

☐ uses evidence from the text.

☐ is written in complete sentences.

Weird and Wondrous ROCKS
by April Pulley Sayre

Notice & Note
Contrasts and Contradictions

Prepare to Read

GENRE STUDY **Poetry** uses the sounds and rhythms of words to show images and express feelings.

- Poems include sound effects, such as rhyme, rhythm, and meter, to reinforce the meaning of the poem.

- Poets include figurative language, such as similes and metaphors, to develop the ideas in their poems.

- A lyric poem expresses the thoughts and feelings of a speaker. A concrete poem uses typeface and shape to reflect a topic or idea.

SET A PURPOSE **Think about** the title and genre of this text. What do you want to learn about natural wonders? Write your ideas below.

Build Background:
Natural Wonders

CRITICAL VOCABULARY

diverse

idle

core

fathom

wrath

collision

Nature's Wonders

Poetry About Our Amazing Earth

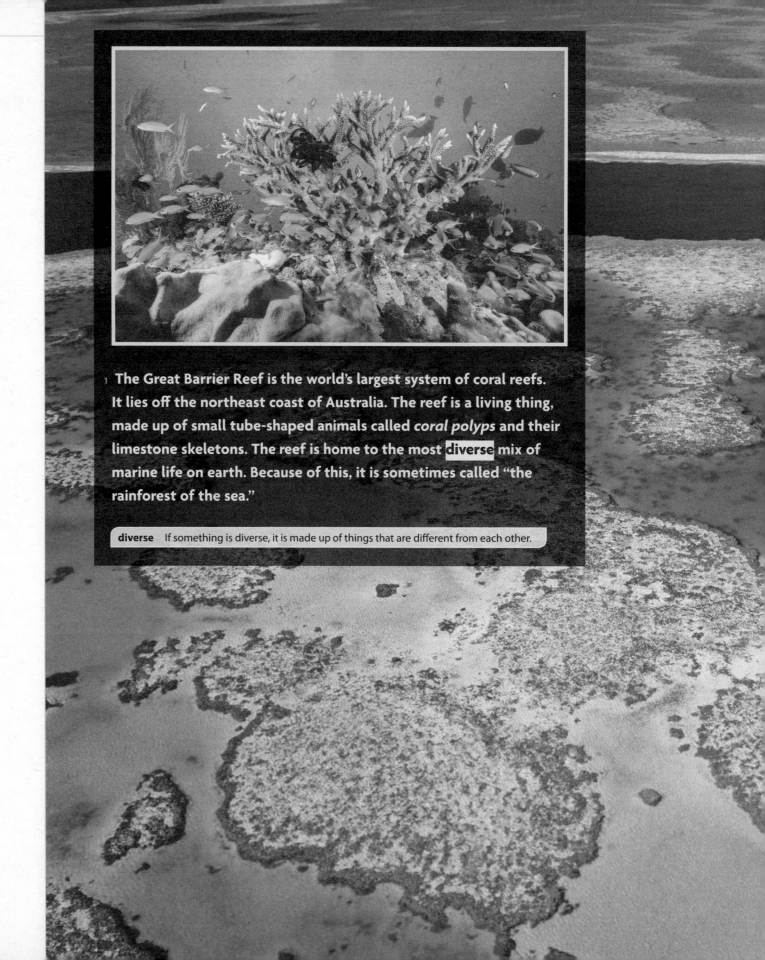

1 **The Great Barrier Reef is the world's largest system of coral reefs. It lies off the northeast coast of Australia. The reef is a living thing, made up of small tube-shaped animals called *coral polyps* and their limestone skeletons. The reef is home to the most diverse mix of marine life on earth. Because of this, it is sometimes called "the rainforest of the sea."**

diverse If something is diverse, it is made up of things that are different from each other.

The Great Barrier Reef

In the Coral Sea, off the coast of Queensland, Australia

2 It's sixteen hundred miles long
along the Queensland coast,
the barrier reef whose name is "Great,"
and that's no idle boast.

3 It's sixteen hundred miles long
and every inch alive.
Perhaps you'd like to have a look?
You do not need to dive

4 or even get your swimsuit wet
to see this awesome place;
the reef's so huge it's visible
by astronauts in space.

5 To think, you can be orbiting
the earth while looking at
a teeming turtle, dolphin, whale
and porpoise habitat.

6 Your eyes will tell the story
and you will not doubt its moral:
There's hardly anything on earth
more beautiful than coral.

—Robert Schechter

idle   If something is referred to as idle, it is not doing anything.
An idle boast is bragging about something that cannot happen.

1 The Mariana Trench is the lowest point in the world. It lies beneath the deep waters of the Pacific Ocean. The first people to explore the Mariana Trench were Don Walsh and Jacques Piccard. They traveled in a steel capsule made to withstand the crushing pressure, tens of thousands of feet below the sea.

The Mariana Trench

Western Pacific Ocean, east of the Mariana Islands

2 In all the oceans, nowhere else so deep,
So dark with secrets men won't let it keep:
It yields to human eyes in submarines
And then, full of itself, goes back to sleep.

3 You wouldn't dream that hidden at its core
Life would go on as it has done for more
Than most of time, though seven heavy miles
Of water press down upon its floor.

4 To fathom it at last, to put on show
All that it holds, laid out in a neat row,
May happen sooner than to do that to
The mind of someone whom you think you know.

—X.J. Kennedy

core The core of something is its center.
fathom If you fathom something, you understand it.

1   Located in the Himalayas in South Asia, Mount Everest is 29,035 feet above sea level, which makes it the highest peak in the world. Everest was formed when the Indian tectonic plate pushed against the Asian plate. Each year, Everest grows a little over an eighth of an inch. This is due to the fact that the Indian plate continues to move against the Asian plate.

2   In the 1920s, British expeditions made multiple attempts to climb to the top of Mount Everest. On May 29th, 1953, Sir Edmund Hillary and Tenzing Norgay were the first recorded people to make it to the summit. However, British explorers George Mallory and Andrew Irvine may have reached the summit first. In 1924, they disappeared while attempting the climb. To this day, no one knows whether or not they made it to the summit.

Mount Everest

Himalaya Mountains, on the border between Tibet and Nepal in Asia

3   Eyes
        travel up
        to the skies,
     following the path
   of the mountain's rise;
    the wind's wrath whips
  through our tents, as my heart skips
 and trips. We hush our fears through the night;
rushing gusts of wind and snow frighten us in jest, as we wait
for that warming sight, the morning light, and continue this quest,
to a point higher than the rest, a height that will be conquered by only the best,
the strength of muscle will be put to test—to climb to the top of Mount Everest.

—Carol R. Baik

wrath   Wrath is strong anger.

1 The shifting, flickering lights of the Aurora Borealis are a wonder to see. The light show of the Aurora Borealis comes from the **collision** between electrically charged particles from the sun as they enter the earth's atmosphere. Typically seen near the northern polar region, some of the best places to view the Aurora Borealis in North America are Alaska and the Canadian Yukon.

Aurora Borealis

2 Over the shores of Labrador
a certain rippling purple curtain
scatters light throughout the night.
(Wait—the color's now a duller
hue of violet-turning-blue!)
This arctic veil, a breaching whale
could peer behind, and still be blind
as anyone. The northern sun
has bent to drape her gauzy cape
across the skies, and left my eyes
to stare and stare at the glittering air.

—Steven Withrow

collision A collision happens when a moving object crashes into something.

52

Collaborative Discussion

Look back at what you wrote on page 46. Tell a partner two things you learned in this text. Then work with a group to discuss the questions below. Use *Nature's Wonders* to support your ideas. Take notes for your responses. When you speak, use your notes.

1 Reread the poem "The Great Barrier Reef." How does the poet feel about the reef? How do you know?

Listening Tip

Listen to each speaker's ideas. What questions do they raise in your mind?

2 Review the poem "Aurora Borealis." What images do the speaker's words create in your mind?

Speaking Tip

Ask questions related to what another speaker has said. Listen carefully to the responses and add your own ideas.

3 How does the informational passage with each poem add to your understanding?

Write a Response

PROMPT

Respond to the Text In *Nature's Wonders,* you read poems and some facts about four natural wonders. How would you describe these natural wonders? What makes them unique? How does the informational text add to what you learn from the poems? Cite evidence from the text to support your response.

EVIDENCE

List details in *Nature's Wonders* that describe each natural wonder and tell why it is unique.

WRITE

Now write your response in a paragraph.

Make sure your response

- ☐ uses evidence from the text to answer the questions.
- ☐ describes the different types of natural wonders in the selection.
- ☐ tells how the informational text adds to the meaning of the poems.
- ☐ is written in complete sentences.

Prepare to Read and View

GENRE STUDY **Literary nonfiction** tells a factually accurate story using literary techniques.

- Literary nonfiction presents events in chronological order.
- Science texts include words that are specific to the topic.
- Authors of literary nonfiction may use figurative language, such as similes and metaphors, to describe real places or events.

SET A PURPOSE **Look through** the images in this selection. What images interest you the most? What would you like to learn about these parts of the Grand Canyon? Write your ideas below.

Meet the Author:
Linda Vieira
Meet the Illustrator:
Christopher Canyon

CRITICAL VOCABULARY

shatter

sentries

chasm

glistens

embedded

eroding

GRAND CANYON

A TRAIL THROUGH TIME

by Linda Vieira

illustrations by

Christopher Canyon

1   A predawn storm rumbles over Grand Canyon National Park. Cracks of lightning shatter the dark sky, flashing above an enormous plateau of peaks, valleys, and trenches where ancient mountains once stood. The deepest trench is called the Grand Canyon, one of the Seven Natural Wonders of the World.

shatter   When things shatter, they explode or suddenly break into pieces.

2   **D**awn comes, bringing daylight to spires and buttes standing like sentries on the plateau, worn down by weathering and erosion. Coyotes teach their pups to hunt for food in thick forests along the edges of the Canyon.

3   Thousands of visitors from all over the world have come to view the splendor of the Grand Canyon. In campgrounds and lodges near the north and south rims, they prepare for the day's activities.

sentries   Sentries are guards or lookouts who stand in a place to keep watch.

59

4 The morning sun climbs above distant mountains, revealing cliffs hanging over the Colorado River at the bottom of the Grand Canyon. The river took almost six million years to carve the Canyon, creating a channel about one mile deep and more than 275 miles long. Wind and water wore down its steep sides, widening the chasm between the cliffs. A raven glides across the opening, making lazy circles over the river far below.

5 The sun chases away shadows on the craggy rocks thousands of feet below the rims. Pack mules begin a five-hour trip down to the deepest part of the Canyon. They follow each other along a twisted, ten-mile trail to the riverbed. Clouds of dust follow them as voices from the top fade away.

chasm   A chasm is a deep crack or opening in the ground.

6   Canyon visitors along the trail peer with curiosity at symbols of people and animals that were painted on a boulder by Havasupai Indians long ago. Havasupai still live in the Canyon today, tending their flocks and farms in the summertime, hunting small game and gathering nuts and berries in the winter months.

7   As the sun moves higher in the sky, smaller side canyons with rocks layered like multicolored ribbons come into view. Bighorn sheep walk easily along the steep walls of the canyons, looking for food in hidden pockets of soil. Wildflowers stand around them in patches of purple and pink.

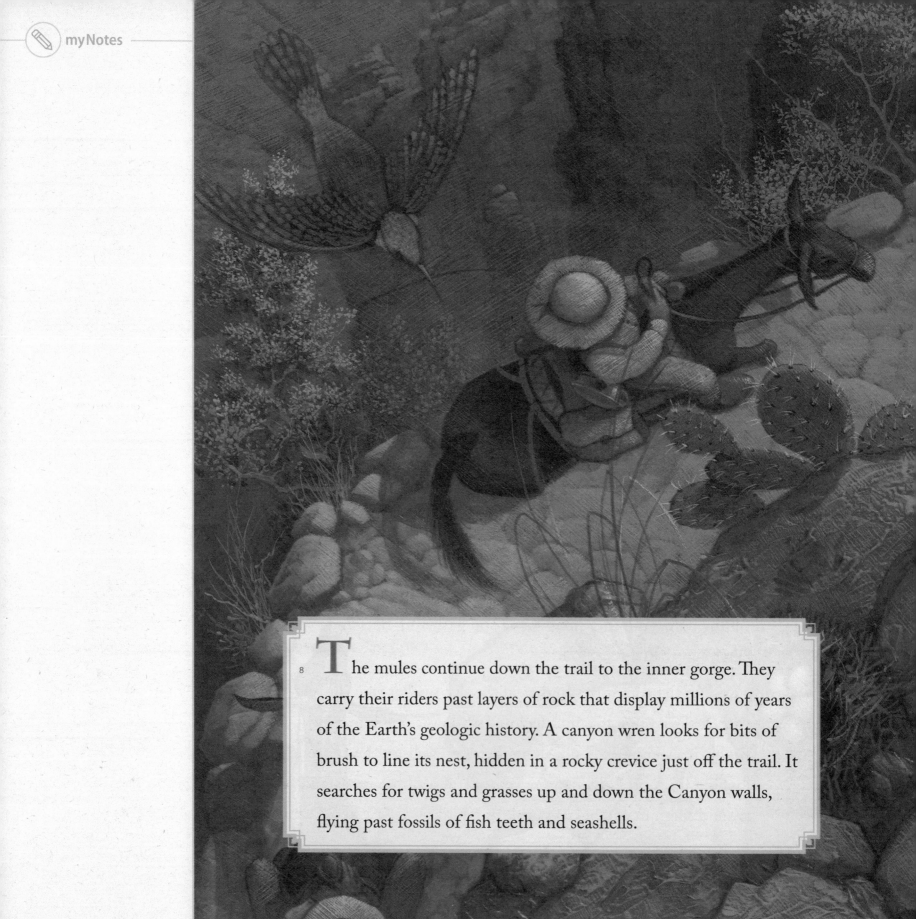

8 The mules continue down the trail to the inner gorge. They carry their riders past layers of rock that display millions of years of the Earth's geologic history. A canyon wren looks for bits of brush to line its nest, hidden in a rocky crevice just off the trail. It searches for twigs and grasses up and down the Canyon walls, flying past fossils of fish teeth and seashells.

9 The noonday sun glistens on a hidden creek near a granary built into the Canyon wall by Anasazi Indians almost 1,000 years ago. Squirrels chase through the now-empty granary, where crops and plants had been stored for food and trade.

10 A lizard scurries off the trail. It climbs over fossils of prehistoric trilobites, embedded in layers of shale millions of years ago when the land was covered by a primeval sea. After the mules pass, the lizard creeps out from its hiding place to soak up the warmth of the sun.

glistens If something glistens, it sparkles or shines.
embedded If a thing is embedded, it is firmly set into something else that surrounds it.

11   The afternoon sun hangs low in the sky. A white-breasted nuthatch flies above beavertail cacti along the rocky banks of the Colorado River. Its song drifts over ancient pink, white, and gray rocks at the river's edge, the roots of mountains that stood there almost two billion years ago. The water tumbles over cascading rapids, while trout search for quieter streams in which to spawn.

12   A ringtail cat drinks from a slower side stream, watching for predators up and down the red rocks and along the river nearby. Laughter echoes from a bunkhouse, as weary riders and hikers share stories of their descent into the Canyon.

13   The endless cycles of eroding rock and moving water carved the Grand Canyon millions of years ago. Blustering wind and pounding rain continue to widen it, grinding down rocks that used to be mountains and volcanoes. The rushing Colorado River deepens this natural wonder, dragging rocks and mud along its path through ancient plains and lava flows.

eroding   If something is eroding, it is slowly wearing away, often from wind or water.

14 The mules rest for the night in a corral near the river, awaiting tomorrow's seven-hour trip back up to the top. Weather and erosion make tiny changes every day in the rocky walls along the trail. Millions of years into the future, the same forces of nature will continue to reshape the Grand Canyon, digging even deeper into the history of our planet.

Collaborative Discussion

Look back at what you wrote on page 56. Tell a partner two things you learned from this text. Take notes to answer the questions below. Refer to details and examples in *Grand Canyon: A Trail Through Time* to explain your answers. Then work with a group to discuss the questions. When you speak, use your notes.

1 Reread page 60. How big is the Grand Canyon? Why did it take so many years to form?

Listening Tip

Don't do all the talking! Notice when others in your group have not shared their opinions and ideas and ask them to do so.

2 What plants and animals might you see living in the Canyon?

Speaking Tip

Add new ideas to the conversation, speaking loudly enough so that everyone can hear easily.

3 How have moving water and erosion worked together to create the Grand Canyon?

Write a Response

PROMPT ....

Respond to the Text In *Grand Canyon: A Trail Through Time,* you read a description of the Grand Canyon, one of the Seven Natural Wonders of the World. What did you learn about the Grand Canyon? How would you describe it? What do visitors to the Grand Canyon experience? Cite evidence from the text to support your response.

EVIDENCE ....

List details in *Grand Canyon: A Trail Through Time* that tell how the Grand Canyon is a unique natural wonder.

GRAND
CANYON

A TRAIL THROUGH TIME

by Linda Vieira

illustrations by
Christopher Canyon

Now write your response in a paragraph.

✓ Make sure your response

- ☐ answers the questions.

- ☐ describes the unique features of the Grand Canyon.

- ☐ tells what visitors to the Grand Canyon experience.

- ☐ uses evidence from the text.

- ☐ is written in complete sentences.

Essential Question

What makes Earth's natural wonders exciting and unique?

Write an Expository Essay

PROMPT Think about what you learned about natural wonders in this module. How would you describe each one? What makes these natural wonders exciting and unique? Use evidence from the texts in this module to write an expository essay about what makes Earth's natural wonders exciting and unique. Use some of the vocabulary words from the module in your writing.

✓ Be sure your expository essay
☐ provides an introduction that states the topic clearly.
☐ supports each central idea with facts, details, and examples from the texts.
☐ groups related information into paragraphs.
☐ uses transition words and phrases, such as *also, in addition, but,* and *however.*
☐ has a conclusion that sums up the information.

.... Map your ideas.

Think about the natural wonders you read about in this module. What makes them exciting and unique? Why? Use the sentence frames below to plan your writing.

_____ is exciting and unique because _____

_____ .

_____

_____

_____ .

_____ is exciting and unique because _____

_____

_____

_____

_____ .

_____ is exciting and unique because _____

_____

_____

_____

_____ .

DRAFT .... Write your expository essay.

Use the information you wrote on page 71 to draft your expository essay. Write a **beginning paragraph** that introduces your topic.

Write several **paragraphs** to describe the natural wonders you read about. Tell what makes them unique. Cite text evidence when describing each one. Use transitions to connect your ideas.

Write a **conclusion** that summarizes your ideas.

REVISE AND EDIT .... Review your draft.

The revising and editing steps give you a chance to look carefully at your draft and make changes. Work with a partner to determine whether you have clearly supported your topic and explained your ideas. Use these questions to help you.

✓ PURPOSE/ FOCUS	ORGANIZATION	EVIDENCE/SUPPORT	ELABORATION	CONVENTIONS
☐ Does my essay answer all the questions?	☐ Do I have a clear introduction to my topic?	☐ Did I include text evidence and examples from the selections?	☐ Did I use transition words to connect ideas?	☐ Have I spelled all the words correctly?
☐ Did I clearly explain what makes the natural wonders exciting and unique?	☐ Did I group related information?		☐ Did I use any module vocabulary words?	☐ Have I used correct punctuation and capitalization?
	☐ Does my conclusion summarize my topic?			☐ Have I included descriptive words and phrases?

PUBLISH .... Create a finished copy.

Make a final copy of your expository essay. Write legibly using your cursive writing skills.

Tricksters and Tall Tales

"There is magic to storytelling."

— Lynn Collins

Essential Question

What lessons can you learn from characters in traditional tales?

Get Curious
Video

Folktale

Traditional Stories

Fable

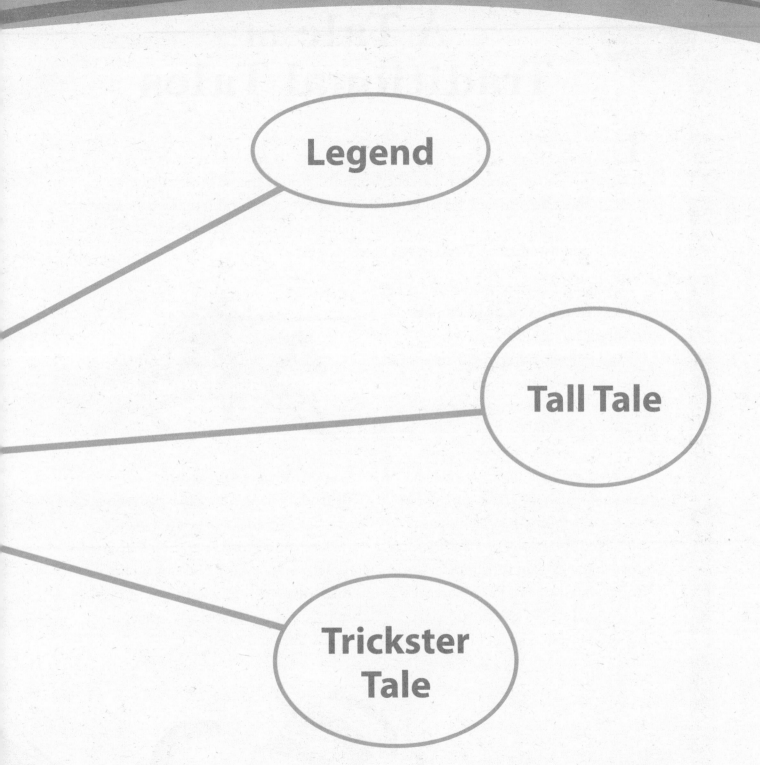

Legend

Tall Tale

Trickster Tale

myNotes

A Tale of Traditional Tales

1 Long ago, people told stories to each other. They shared tales of great heroes, of larger-than-life characters, of great adventures. People shared these tales with their children, friends, and neighbors. The stories were told and retold for hundreds or even thousands of years. Today, we still enjoy these stories in our libraries, in our classrooms, and on TV and movie screens.

2 Folktales, legends, myths, and other traditional stories all share a timeless quality. That means these tales, no matter how old, never lose their appeal. Their plots and themes continue to entertain people and teach valuable lessons about life.

3 Before reading and writing were invented, storytelling was a vital way to share information. Traditional stories often gave explanations for things people wondered about long ago. For example, a story might explain why thunderstorms happen or why bears have short tails. Traditional stories also provided important lessons about life. They might dazzle listeners with accounts of legendary battles or fearless adventurers. Traditional stories preserved people's values and history. And they were always entertaining. Many traditional tales included repetition. Repeated lines and phrases made these stories easier to remember and retell.

78

4   Today, we still share ancient traditional stories because of the lessons, or morals, they teach about life. The famous fables of the ancient Greek storyteller Aesop are often about animals, but they include morals that humans would be wise to keep in mind. In Aesop's "The Ants and the Grasshopper," hardworking ants gather food for the winter while their friend the grasshopper lazes about. When winter comes, however, the grasshopper has to beg the ants to share their food. The lesson seems clear and makes sense even today: Work hard and plan for the future—or else!

5   Traditional tales usually feature characters with traits we all can recognize. Some are wise, some are silly, some are greedy, and some are generous. The stories include **exaggeration** not only to entertain us but also to draw attention to extraordinary behavior. Larger-than-life traits hold a mirror to real human behavior. They teach readers the value of virtue and the dangers of acting badly.

6   One type of exaggerated character is the **trickster.** The trickster is usually a **shrewd**, or clever, fun-loving animal character who loves to play tricks on others. Sometimes, the trickster is the one who gets tricked. Either way, the trickster always teaches a valuable lesson.

7   The humor and life lessons in traditional tales make them just as relevant today as they were long ago and will be in the future. Which one is your favorite?

Notice & Note
Again and Again

Prepare to Read

GENRE STUDY **Tall tales** are exaggerated stories that are meant to be entertaining.

- Tall tales include a main character who is larger than life and who often has super-human abilities.
- The main character in a tall tale solves problems in a funny way that is hard to believe.
- Authors of tall tales use exaggerated descriptions of characters and events.

SET A PURPOSE **Think about** what you know about tall tales. What are some things you'd like to know about the main character in this story? Write your ideas below.

Meet the Author:
Jerdine Nolen
Meet the Illustrator:
Kadir Nelson

CRITICAL VOCABULARY

recall

vividly

accentuated

partial

splendor

resourceful

disposition

commendable

devastation

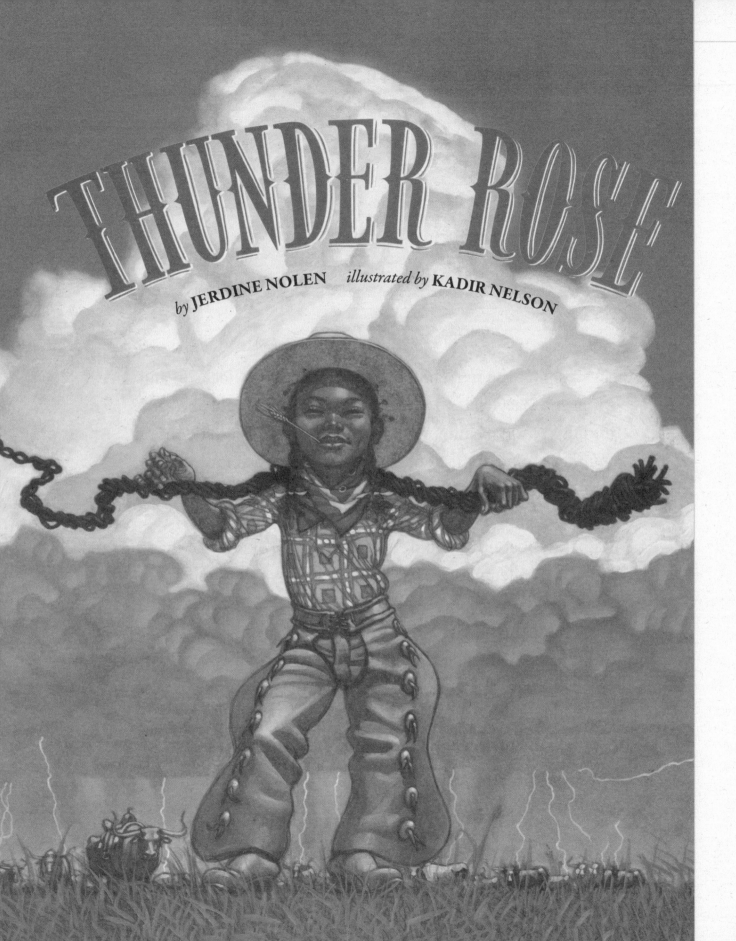

THUNDER ROSE

by **JERDINE NOLEN**   *illustrated by* **KADIR NELSON**

1   Rose was the first child born free and easy to Jackson and Millicent MacGruder. I recall most vividly the night she came into this world. Hailing rain, flashing lightning, and booming thunder pounded the door, inviting themselves in for the blessed event.

2   Taking in her first breath of life, the infant did not cry out. Rather, she sat up and looked around. She took hold of that lightning, rolled it into a ball, and set it above her shoulder, while the thunder echoed out over the other. They say this just accentuated the fact that the child had the power of thunder and lightning coursing through her veins.

3   "She's going to grow up to be good and strong, all right," Doc Hollerday said.

4   The child turned to the good doctor with a thoughtful glance and replied, "I reckon I will want to do more than that. Thank you very kindly!"

---

recall   If you recall something, you tell about something you remember.
vividly   If you remember something vividly, you have a clear, detailed memory of it.
accentuated   If something is accentuated, it has attention drawn to it.

5   Shifting her gaze to the two loving lights shining on her, which were her ma and pa, she remarked, "Much obliged to you both for this chance to make my way in the world!" Then she announced to no one in particular, "I am right partial to the name Rose."

6   So much in love with this gift of their lives, her ma and pa hovered over her in watchful splendor. Overcome with that love, they lifted their voices in song, an old song and a melody so sweet and true—a lullaby passed down from the ages, echoing since the beginning of time.

---

partial   If you are partial to something, you prefer it more than other things.
splendor   The splendor of something is its great beauty or impressive appearance.

7   "There is a music ringing so sweetly in my ears," the newborn exclaimed. "It's giving me a fortunate feeling rumbling deep in the pit of me. I'll register it here at the bull's-eye set in the center of my heart, and see what I can do with it one day!"

8   Rose snored up plenty that first night breathing on her own, rattling the rafters on the roof right along with the booming thunder. There was nothing quiet about her slumber. She seemed determined to be just as forceful as that storm. With the thunder and lightning keeping watch over her the rest of the night, her ma and pa just took to calling her Thunder Rose.

9   The next morning, when the sun was high yellow in that billowy blue sky, Rose woke up hungry as a bear in spring, but not the least bit ornery. Minding her manners, she politely thanked her ma for the milk, but it was not enough to quench her hungry thirst. Rose preferred, instead, to drink her milk straight from the cow.

10   Her ma was right grateful to have such a resourceful child. No other newborn had the utter strength to lift a whole cow clear over her head and almost drink it dry. In a moment's time, Rose did, and quite daintily so. She was as pretty as a picture, had the sweetest disposition, but don't let yourself be misled, that child was full of lightning *and* thunder.

11   Out on that paper-bag brown, dusty dry, wide-open space, Rose often was found humming a sweet little tune as she did her chores. And true to her word, Rose did *more* than grow good and strong.

12   The two-year-old became quite curious about the pile of scrap iron lying next to the barn. Rose took a good-sized piece, stretched it here, bent and twisted it there. She constructed a thunderbolt as black as pitch to punctuate her name. She called it Cole. Wherever she went, Cole was always by her side. Noticing how skilled Rose was with the metal, her pa made sure there was an extra supply of it always around.

13   At the age of five, Rose did a commendable job of staking the fence without a bit of help. During her eighth and ninth years, Rose assembled some iron beams together with the wood blocks she used to play with and constructed a building tall enough to scrape the sky, always humming as she worked.

14   By the time she turned twelve, Rose had perfected her metal-bending practices. She formed delicately shaped alphabet letters to help the young ones learn to read.

---

resourceful   If you are resourceful, you are good at solving problems quickly.
disposition   Your disposition is the way you tend to act or feel.
commendable   If you do something commendable, you do it well and earn praise.

For his birthday, Rose presented her pa with a branding iron,
a circle with a big *M-A-C* for MacGruder in the middle, just
in time, too, because a herd of quick-tempered longhorn steer
was stampeding its way up from the Rio Grande. They were
plowing a path straight toward her front door.

15   Rose performed an eye-catching wonder, the likes of which
was something to see. Running lightning-fast toward the
herd, using Cole for support, Rose vaulted into the air and
landed on the back of the biggest lead steer like he was a
merry-go-round pony. Grabbing a horn in each hand, Rose
twisted that varmint to a complete halt. It was just enough to
restrain that top bull and the rest of the herd.

16   But I believe what touched that critter's heart was when Rose began humming her little tune. That cantankerous ton of beef was restless no more. He became as playful as a kitten and even tried to purr. Rose named him Tater on account of that was his favorite vegetable. Hearing Rose's lullaby put that considerable creature to sleep was the sweetest thing I had witnessed in a long, long time.

17   After the dust had settled, Ma and Pa counted twenty-seven hundred head of cattle, after they added in the five hundred they already had. Using the scrap iron, Rose had to add a new section to the bull pen to hold them all.

18   "What did you do to the wire, Rose?" Ma asked, surprised and pleased at her daughter's latest creation.

19   "Oh, that," she said. "While I was staking the fence, Pa asked me to keep little Barbara Jay company. That little twisty pattern seemed to make the baby laugh. So I like to think of it as Barbara's Wire."

20   "That was right clever of you to be so entertaining to the little one like that!" her ma said. Rose just blushed. Over the years, that twisty wire caught on, and folks just called it barbed wire.

89

21   Rose and her pa spent the whole next day sorting the animals that had not been branded. "One day soon, before the cold weather gets in," she told her pa, "I'll have to get this herd up the Chisholm Trail and to market in Abilene. I suspect Tater is the right kind of horse for the long drive northward."

22   On Rose's first trip to Abilene, while right outside of Caldwell, that irascible, full-of-outrage-and-ire outlaw Jesse Baines and his gang of desperadoes tried to rustle that herd away from Rose.

23   Using the spare metal rods she always carried with her, Rose lassoed those hot-tempered hooligans up good and tight. She dropped them all off to jail, tied up in a nice neat iron bow. "It wasn't any trouble at all," she told Sheriff Weaver. "Somebody had to put a stop to their thieving ways."

24   But that wasn't the only thieving going on. The mighty sun was draining the moisture out of every living thing it touched. Even the rocks were crying out. Those clouds stood by and watched it all happen. They weren't even trying to be helpful.

25   Why, the air had turned so dry and sour, time seemed to all but stand still. And there was not a drop of water in sight. Steer will not move without water. And that was making those bulls mad, real mad. And when a bull gets angry, it's like a disease that's catching, making the rest of the herd mad, too. Tater was looking parched and mighty thirsty.

26   "I've got to do something about this!" Rose declared.

27   Stretching out several iron rods lasso-fashion, then launching Cole high in the air, Rose hoped she could get the heavens to yield forth. She caught hold of a mass of clouds and squeezed them hard, real hard, all the while humming her song. Gentle rain began to fall. But anyone looking could see there was not enough moisture to refresh two ants, let alone a herd of wild cows.

28   Suddenly a rotating column of air came whirling and swirling around, picking up everything in its path. It sneaked up on Rose. "Whoa, there, now just hold on a minute," Rose called out to the storm. Tater was helpless to do anything about that sort of wind. Those meddlesome clouds caused it. They didn't take kindly to someone telling them what to do. And they were set on creating a riotous rampage all on their own.

29   Oh, this riled Rose so much, she became the only two-legged tempest to walk the western plains. "You don't know who you're fooling with," Rose called out to the storm. Her eyes flashed lightning. She bit down and gnashed thunder from her teeth. I don't know why anyone would want to mess with a pretty young woman who had the power of thunder and lightning coursing through her veins. But, pity for them, the clouds did!

30   Rose reached for her iron rod. But there was only one piece left. She did not know which way to turn. She knew Cole

alone was not enough to do the job right. Unarmed against her own growing thirst and the might of the elements, Rose felt weighted down. Then that churning column split, and now there were two. They were coming at her from opposite directions. Rose had some fast thinking to do. Never being one to bow down under pressure, she considered her options, for she was not sure how this would all come out in the end.

31   "Is this the fork in the road with which I have my final supper? Will this be my first and my last ride of the roundup?" she queried herself in the depths of her heart. Her contemplations brought her little relief as she witnessed the merciless, the cataclysmic efforts of a windstorm bent on her disaster. Then the winds joined hands and cranked and churned a path heading straight toward her! Calmly Rose spoke out loud to the storm as she stood alone to face the wrack and ruin, the multiplying devastation. "I *could* ride at least *one* of you out to the end of time! But I've got this fortunate feeling rumbling deep in the pit of me, and I see what I am to do with it this day!" Rose said, smiling.

devastation   Devastation is terrible damage or complete destruction.

32   The winds belted at a rumbling pitch. Rose squarely faced that storm. "Come and join me, winds!" She opened her arms wide as if to embrace the torrent. She opened her mouth as if she were planning to take a good long drink. But from deep inside her, she heard a melody so real and sweet and true. And when she lifted her heart, she unleashed *her* song of thunder. It was a sight to see: Rose making thunder and lightning rise and fall to the ground at her command, at the sound of *her song*. Oh, how her voice rang out so clear and real and true. It rang from the mountaintops. It filled up the valleys. It flowed like a healing river in the breathing air around her.

33   Those tornadoes, calmed by her song, stopped their
churning masses and raged no more. And, gentle as a baby's
bath, a soft, drenching-and-soaking rain fell.

34   And Rose realized that by reaching into her own heart to
bring forth the music that was there, she had even touched
the hearts of the clouds.

35   The stories of Rose's amazing abilities spread like wildfire,
far and wide. And as sure as thunder follows lightning, and
sun follows rain, whenever you see a spark of light flash
across a heavy steel gray sky, listen to the sound of the
thunder and think of Thunder Rose and *her* song. That
mighty, mighty song pressing on the bull's-eye that was set at
the center of her heart.

Collaborative Discussion

Look back at what you wrote on page 80. Tell a partner two things you learned about Rose. Then work with a group to discuss the questions below. Refer to details from *Thunder Rose*. Take notes for your responses. When you speak, use your notes.

1 Review pages 82–83. What is unusual about Rose on the night she is born?

2 What events in the story show that Rose is a larger-than-life character?

3 Review pages 92–96. What does Rose do to stop the two tornadoes? How is she able to do this?

Listening Tip

Listen to each speaker's ideas. What detail or example can you add?

Speaking Tip

Restate a speaker's idea and share another detail or example that is related to it.

Write a Response

PROMPT ·

Respond to the Text In *Thunder Rose*, you read a tall tale about a larger-than-life character who does incredible things. Think about Rose's character traits and actions. How would you describe her? How does Rose solve problems? Cite evidence from the text to support your response. Try to use some of the Critical Vocabulary words in your response.

EVIDENCE ·

List ideas from *Thunder Rose* that show what Rose is like. Note how Rose solves problems in this tall tale.

WRITE

Now write your response in a paragraph.

✓ Make sure your response

- ☐ answers the questions.
- ☐ describes Rose's character traits and actions.
- ☐ explains how Rose solves problems.
- ☐ cites evidence from the tall tale.
- ☐ is written in complete sentences.

myNotes

otice &
Note
Aha Moment

Prepare to Read

GENRE STUDY **Folktales** are traditional stories that have been passed down from one generation to another.

- Folktales include the beliefs and ideas of a culture.
- Authors of folktales tell the story through the plot—the main events of the story. The plot includes a conflict, or problem, and the resolution.
- Folktales include a moral, or lesson learned.

SET A PURPOSE **Think about** the title and the genre of this folktale. What would you like to find out about the characters in this story? Write your ideas below.

CRITICAL VOCABULARY

thrifty

generous

character

fascinated

Meet the Author:
Joe Hayes

In the Days of KING ADOBE

as told by Joe Hayes
illustrated by Ute Simon

1   **T**here was once an old woman who lived all alone in a tiny house at the edge of a village. She was very poor, and all she had to eat was beans and tortillas and thin cornmeal mush. Of course, she ate a few vegetables from her garden, but most of them she took into the village on market day to sell or trade for what little she needed for her simple life.

2   But the old woman was very thrifty, and by saving carefully—a penny a day, a penny a day—she was able to buy herself a big ham. She kept it hanging from a hook in a cool, dark closet behind the kitchen, and she only cut a thin slice from the ham on very special days—or if she was lucky enough to have company join her for a meal.

> **thrifty**   If you are thrifty, you save your money and buy only what you need.

3 One evening a couple of young men who were traveling through the country stopped at the old woman's house and asked if they could have lodging for the night. The old woman had no extra beds, but she offered to spread a blanket on the floor for the young men to sleep on. They said that would be fine and thanked the old woman for her kindness.

4 "It's nothing," the old woman told them. "I'm happy to have the company. I'll get busy and make us all a good supper."

5 She got out her pots and pans and then went to the closet and cut three slices from the ham—two thick, generous slices for the travelers and a thin one for herself.

6 The young men were delighted to see the old woman preparing ham for their supper. Seldom were they offered such good food in their travels. But those two young men were a couple of rascals, and right away a roguish idea came into their minds. They decided to steal the ham that night while the old woman was asleep.

generous   A generous amount of something is larger or more plentiful than is usual or necessary.

7   After they had all eaten their fill, the old woman spread out a bed for the young men on the floor. She said good night and wished them good dreams and then went into her own room to sleep.

8   Of course, the young men didn't go to sleep. They lay on the floor joking and talking about how nice it was going to be to have a whole ham to eat. When they felt sure the old woman was asleep, the young men got up and crept to the closet. They took the ham down from the hook and wrapped it in a shirt. One of the young men put the ham in his traveling bag. Then the two young men lay down to sleep with smiles on their faces. They had very good dreams indeed!

9 But the old woman hadn't gone to sleep either. In the many years of her life she had become a good judge of character, and she had noticed the rascally look in the young men's eyes. She knew she had better be on her guard. When she heard the young men getting up from their pad on the floor, she went to the door and peeked out. She saw everything the young men did.

10 Later that night, when the young men were sound asleep, the old woman crept from her room. She took the ham from the traveling bag and hid it under her bed. Then she wrapped an adobe brick in the shirt and put it in the traveling bag.

11 When the young men awoke in the morning they were anxious to be on their way. But the old woman insisted they stay for a bite of breakfast. "It will give you strength," she told them. "You have a long day of walking ahead of you. And you may not have anything else to eat all day."

> **character** A person's character is the kind of person he or she is.

12   One of the young men winked at the other as he sat down at the table and said, "You're probably right, *abuelita*, but who knows? Last night I dreamed that today my friend and I would be eating good food all day long."

13   "Is that right?" the old woman replied. "Tell me more about your dream. I'm fascinated by dreams. I believe they are sometimes true."

14   The young man thought he'd really make fun of the old woman. He smiled at his friend and then said, "I dreamed we were sitting under a tree eating. It was in a beautiful land. And the king of that country was named Hambone the First."

15   "Aha!" spoke up the second young man. "Now I remember that I had the same dream. And I remember that the land in which Hambone the First was king was named Travelibag."

16   The young men had to cover their mouths to keep from bursting out laughing. But the old woman didn't seem to notice. In fact, she seemed to be taking them very seriously.

17   "I had a similar dream last night myself!" she exclaimed. "I was in a land named Travelibag, and Hambone the First was king of that country. But then he was thrown out by the good people and replaced by a new king named Adobe the Great. And for some people, that meant a time of great hunger had begun."

fascinated   If you are fascinated by something, you are very interested in it.

18   "Isn't that interesting," the young men said, biting their lips to keep from laughing. "Oh, well, it was just a dream." They hurried to finish their breakfast and then went on their way, laughing at the old woman's foolishness.

19   All morning long the two rascals joked about the old woman as they traveled down the road. As midday approached, they began to grow tired. They sat down under a shady tree to rest.

20   "Well, now," said the first young man as he leaned back and closed his eyes. "Don't you think it's time for dreams to come true? Here we are sitting under a tree, just as I dreamed. Open up the land of Travelibag. My stomach tells me I need to visit the king of that land."

21 "By all means," said the other. "Let's see how things are going with our old friend Hambone the First."

22 The young man opened his bag and pulled out the bundle wrapped in his shirt. Chuckling to himself he slowly unwrapped the shirt. Suddenly the smile disappeared from the young man's face. "Oh, no," he gasped. "The old woman knew more about dreams than we thought."

23 "What do you mean?" asked the other.

24 "Well," he said, "she told us Hambone the First had been thrown out, didn't she?"

25 "Yes."

26 "And do you remember who was put in his place?"

27 The young man laughed. "Adobe the Great! Where do you suppose she came up with a name like that?"

28 "Probably right here," said his friend. "Look."

29 The first young man opened his eyes. "I see what you mean," he groaned. "And I see what the old woman meant about the time of great hunger beginning. I'm starved!"

30 After several hungry days the two young men met another kind old woman who fed them a good meal. This time they didn't even think about trying to play any tricks.

Collaborative Discussion

Look back at what you wrote on page 100. Tell a partner two things you liked about this folktale. Then work with a group to discuss the questions below. Refer to details and examples in *In the Days of King Adobe* to explain your answers. Take notes for your responses. When you speak, use your notes.

1 Reread page 102. What clues does the author give that tell you what the old woman's life is like?

Listening Tip

Listen for important points that other speakers make and the evidence they use to support those ideas.

2 Review pages 106–107. What goal does each character have for sharing his or her dream?

Speaking Tip

After a speaker presents an idea and evidence, restate it and tell why you agree or disagree.

3 What details in the text suggest that the old woman is clever?

Write a Response

PROMPT

Respond to the Text   *In the Days of King Adobe* is a folktale that tells the story of two young men who try to trick a kind woman. Think about each character's traits and actions. What happens to each character? What lessons do these characters' actions teach about life? Cite evidence from the text to support your response.

EVIDENCE

List ideas from *In the Days of King Adobe* that describe each character's traits and actions. Note the lessons these characters' actions teach about life.

WRITE

Now write your response in a paragraph.

Make sure your response

☐	answers the questions.
☐	uses details from the folktale.
☐	describes the characters.
☐	explains the lessons learned from the characters' actions.
☐	is written in complete sentences.

Notice &
Note
Again and Again

Prepare to Read

GENRE STUDY A **fable** is a short story meant to teach a lesson. **Trickster tales** are imaginative stories in which one character tricks another character.

- Fables teach a lesson, called a *moral,* that people should apply to their lives. Sometimes the moral is stated at the end of the fable.

- Characters in fables are usually animals.

- Trickster tales include a clever character who knows more than he or she lets on.

SET A PURPOSE **Look at** the pictures of the characters in the two stories. What are some things you would like to know about these characters? Write your ideas below.

Build Background:
Trickster Tales

CRITICAL VOCABULARY

succulent

clamped

A Pair of Tricksters

illustrated by
Maribel Lechuga and *Jui Ishida*

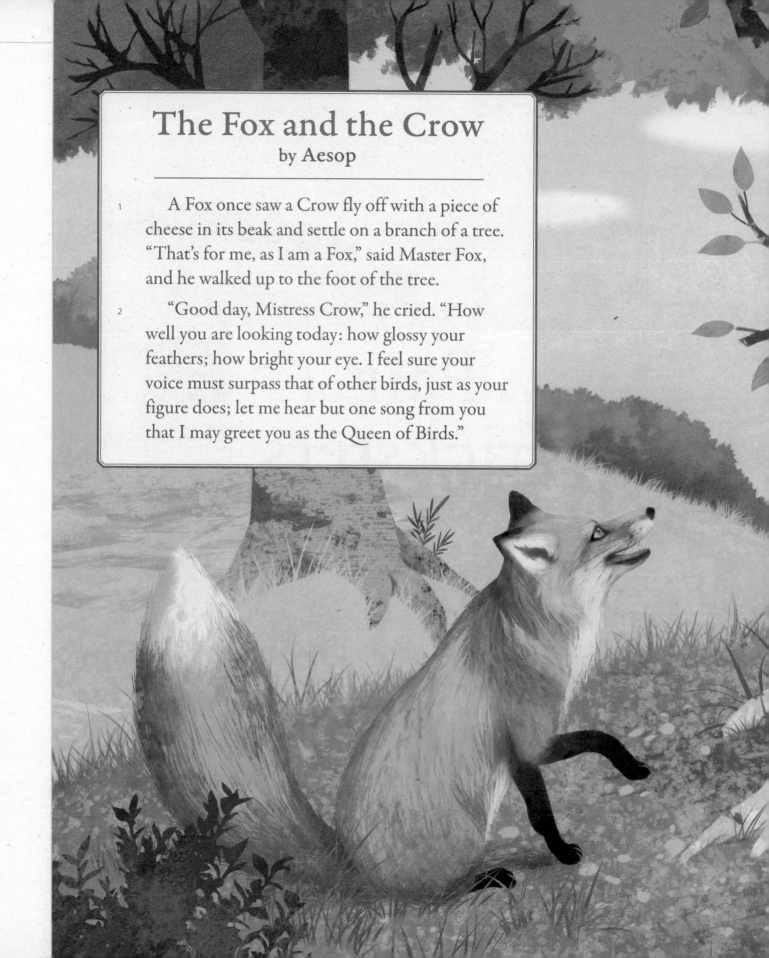

The Fox and the Crow
by Aesop

1   A Fox once saw a Crow fly off with a piece of cheese in its beak and settle on a branch of a tree. "That's for me, as I am a Fox," said Master Fox, and he walked up to the foot of the tree.

2   "Good day, Mistress Crow," he cried. "How well you are looking today: how glossy your feathers; how bright your eye. I feel sure your voice must surpass that of other birds, just as your figure does; let me hear but one song from you that I may greet you as the Queen of Birds."

3   The Crow lifted up her head and began to caw her best, but the moment she opened her mouth the piece of cheese fell to the ground, only to be snapped up by Master Fox.

4   "That will do," said he. "That was all I wanted. In exchange for your cheese I will give you a piece of advice for the future.

5   *Do not trust flatterers.*"

Raven and Crayfish

by John and Caitlín Matthews

1   Flying home to his nest one day, Raven spied a succulent crayfish swimming in the lake below. He swooped down and caught the fat crayfish in his beak, thinking of the feast he would have when he came to his treetop home.

2   Crayfish was terrified. Knowing that she was seconds away from becoming a raven's dinner, she began to speak as calmly and sweetly as she could: "Oh, great and powerful Raven! I'm so pleased to meet you. You know, I had supper with your father and mother a little while ago. What a delightful couple!"

3   "Ugoo," said Raven, because his beak was firmly shut, holding tight to his dinner.

4   "And I have often noticed how enchanting your brothers and sisters are. What a handsome family!" continued Crayfish.

> **succulent**   If food is succulent, it is juicy and tasty.

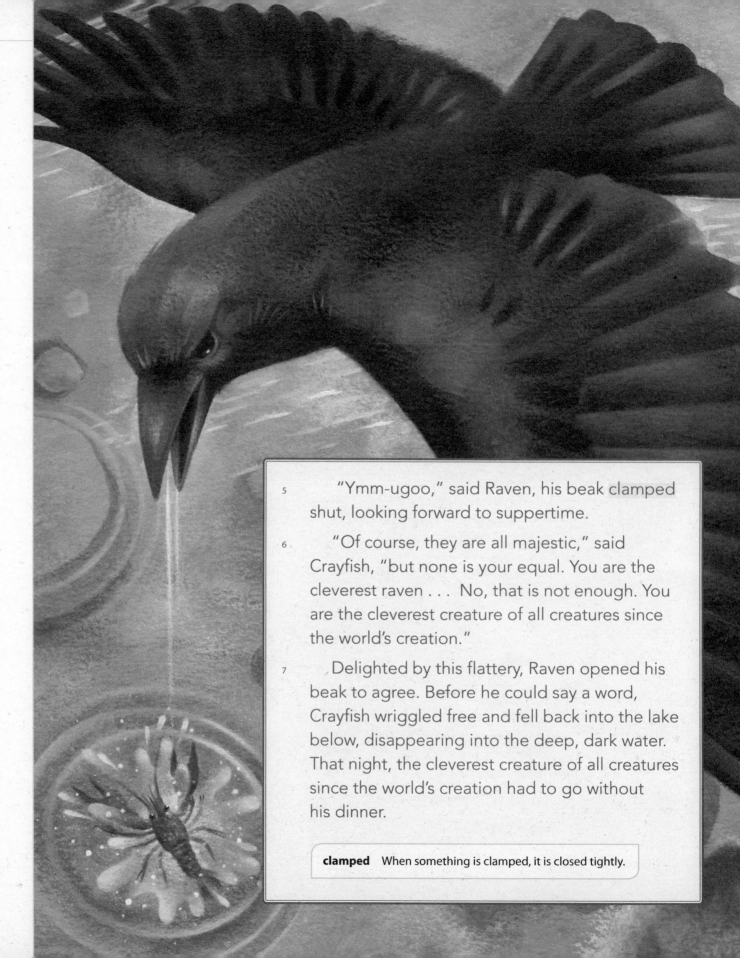

5   "Ymm-ugoo," said Raven, his beak clamped shut, looking forward to suppertime.

6   "Of course, they are all majestic," said Crayfish, "but none is your equal. You are the cleverest raven . . . No, that is not enough. You are the cleverest creature of all creatures since the world's creation."

7   Delighted by this flattery, Raven opened his beak to agree. Before he could say a word, Crayfish wriggled free and fell back into the lake below, disappearing into the deep, dark water. That night, the cleverest creature of all creatures since the world's creation had to go without his dinner.

> **clamped**   When something is clamped, it is closed tightly.

Collaborative Discussion

Look back at what you wrote on page 112. Tell a partner two things you learned about the characters. Then work with a group to discuss the questions below. Refer to details and examples in *A Pair of Tricksters* to explain your answers. Take notes for your responses. When you speak, use your notes.

1. Reread page 114. What do you learn about Fox from what he says to Crow?

2. Review pages 116–118. Who does Crayfish talk about first? Why does she call Raven "the cleverest creature of all creatures"?

3. In what ways are these two stories alike? In what ways are they different?

Listening Tip

Think about the conclusions you can draw from what another speaker has said. Does the speaker's statement change or support your ideas?

Speaking Tip

Say each word clearly and use complete sentences and correct grammar when expressing ideas and supported opinions.

Write a Response

PROMPT ....

Respond to the Text In *A Pair of Tricksters*, you read two versions of a fable in which two characters learn a valuable lesson. Think about the characters' actions in each fable. How are these tales alike and different? What lessons do they teach? Cite evidence from the text to support your response.

EVIDENCE ....

List ideas from *A Pair of Tricksters* that show the lesson learned by the character in each fable.

WRITE

Now write your response in a paragraph.

✓ **Make sure your response**

☐ answers the questions.

☐ uses details from each fable.

☐ describes the characters.

☐ explains the lesson that Crow and Raven learn and how they learn it.

☐ is written in complete sentences.

Notice & Note
Aha Moment

Prepare to Read and View

GENRE STUDY **Legends** are stories from the past that are believed by many people but cannot be proved to be true. Legends may explain how things came to be.

- The main character is known as the hero. The plot includes the hero overcoming an obstacle.
- Events or characters have a larger-than-life quality.

The Ten Suns

Fictional videos tell stories in visual and audio form. A narrator tells the tale while images on the screen support the story.

SET A PURPOSE **Think about** the title and genre of this text and video. What do you think they will be about? How do you think the text and the video will differ? Write your ideas below.

Meet the Author:
Eric A. Kimmel
Meet the Illustrator:
Yongsheng Xuan

CRITICAL VOCABULARY

gratitude

withered

scorching

reckless

assumed

prosper

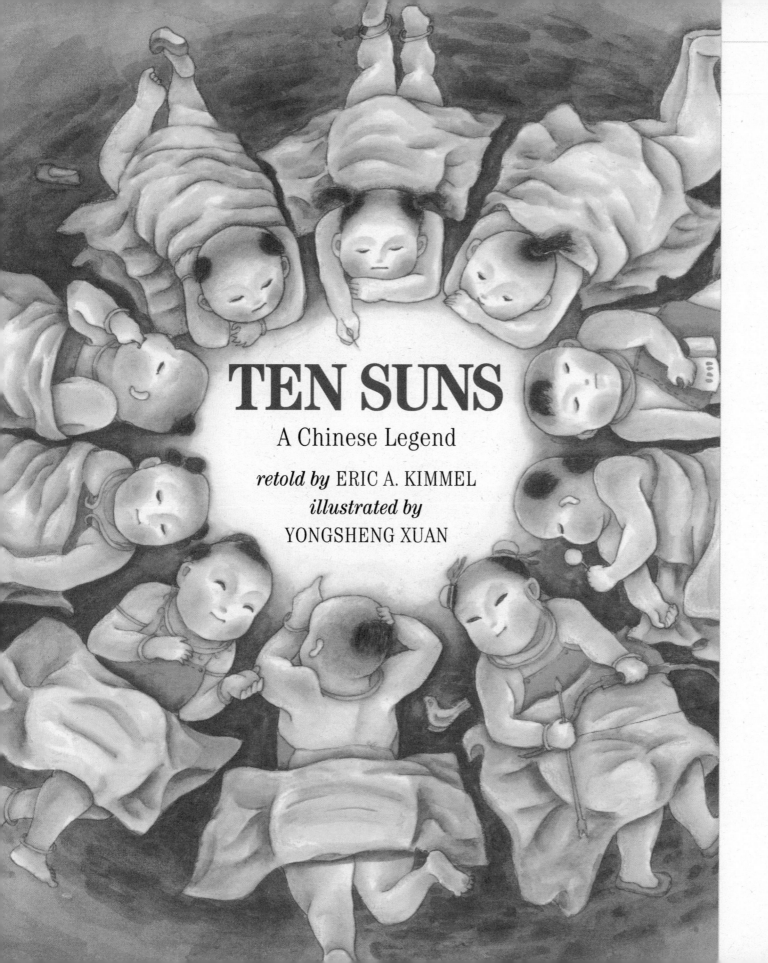

TEN SUNS

A Chinese Legend

retold by ERIC A. KIMMEL

illustrated by
YONGSHENG XUAN

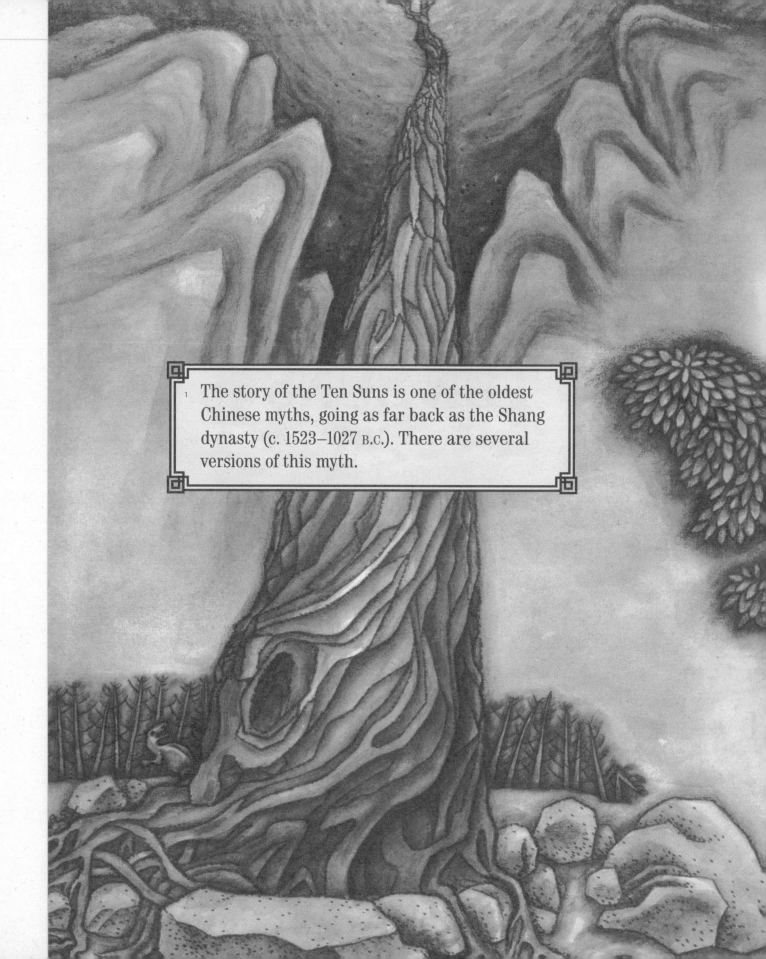

The story of the Ten Suns is one of the oldest Chinese myths, going as far back as the Shang dynasty (c. 1523–1027 B.C.). There are several versions of this myth.

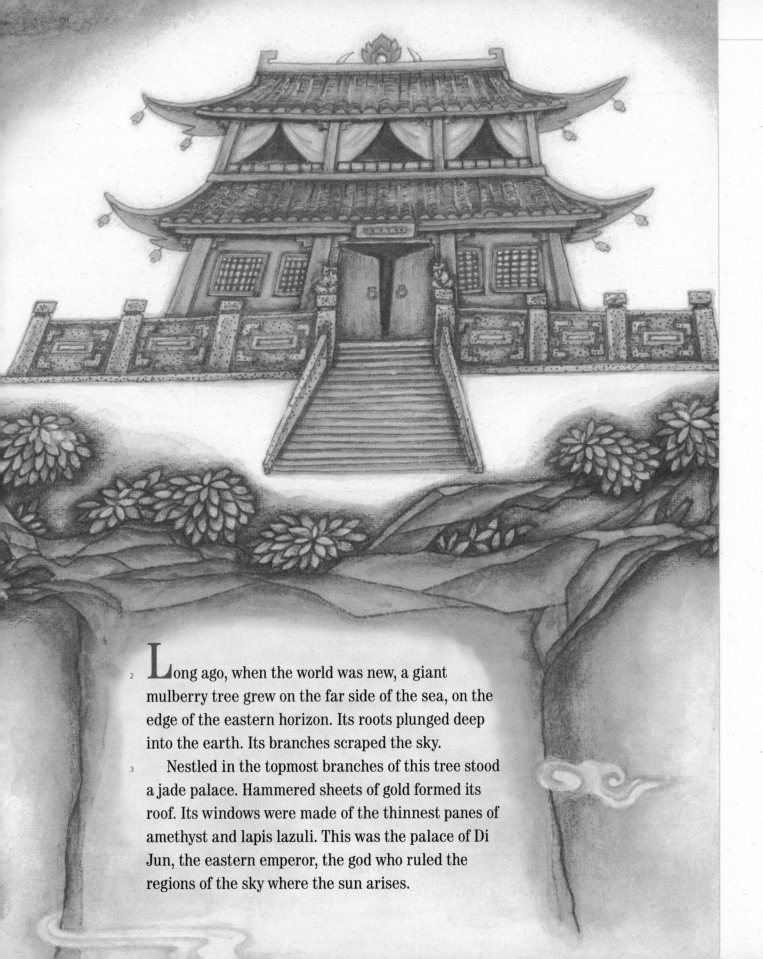

2   Long ago, when the world was new, a giant
mulberry tree grew on the far side of the sea, on the
edge of the eastern horizon. Its roots plunged deep
into the earth. Its branches scraped the sky.

3   Nestled in the topmost branches of this tree stood
a jade palace. Hammered sheets of gold formed its
roof. Its windows were made of the thinnest panes of
amethyst and lapis lazuli. This was the palace of Di
Jun, the eastern emperor, the god who ruled the
regions of the sky where the sun arises.

4   In those days there were ten suns: the children of Di Jun
and his wife, Xi He. They never walked across the sky
together. That would produce too much heat for the world to
bear. Instead, every morning before dawn, Xi He would
awaken one of her sons. They would climb into her dragon
chariot and drive to a point on the eastern horizon where
Xi He's son would begin his walk.

5   Each day one of the suns would walk across the sky from
east to west. When the people on earth saw the sun crossing
the heavens, bringing warmth and light, they offered thanks
to Di Jun, Xi He, and their family.

6   But the gratitude of the earth's people and the importance of their work meant nothing to the boys. They found their task boring. Day after day, year after year, century after century, they followed the same path across the sky. There was no one to talk to, nothing new to see, nothing to do except follow that same weary track over and over again.

gratitude   When you show gratitude, you show that you are thankful.

7   One night, as Di Jun's boys lay in bed, they began talking. Huo Feng Huang, the oldest, said, "I would not mind walking the path so much if I had some company."

8   "I feel the same way," Pi Li Xing, the youngest, replied. "Tomorrow, let's do something different. Why don't we all get up early, take the dragon chariot, and walk across the sky together?"

9   The others agreed. "A splendid idea!"

10   In the dark of night, while their parents slept, the boys arose, put on their brightest garments, hitched the dragon to their mother's chariot, and rode across the star-swept sky to the eastern horizon. Laughing, chattering, with their arms around one another's shoulders, they began their walk.

11   When dawn came, the people who lived on earth were astonished to see ten suns appear above the horizon. The blazing heat of ten suns shining down at once was more than the world could bear. Crops withered in the fields. Forests caught fire. Lakes and rivers dried up. Mountains shattered to pieces. The sea began to boil. People and animals grew faint. They stretched themselves on the scorching ground and waited to die.

withered   If a plant has withered, it has dried up and died.
scorching   Something that is scorching is very, very hot.

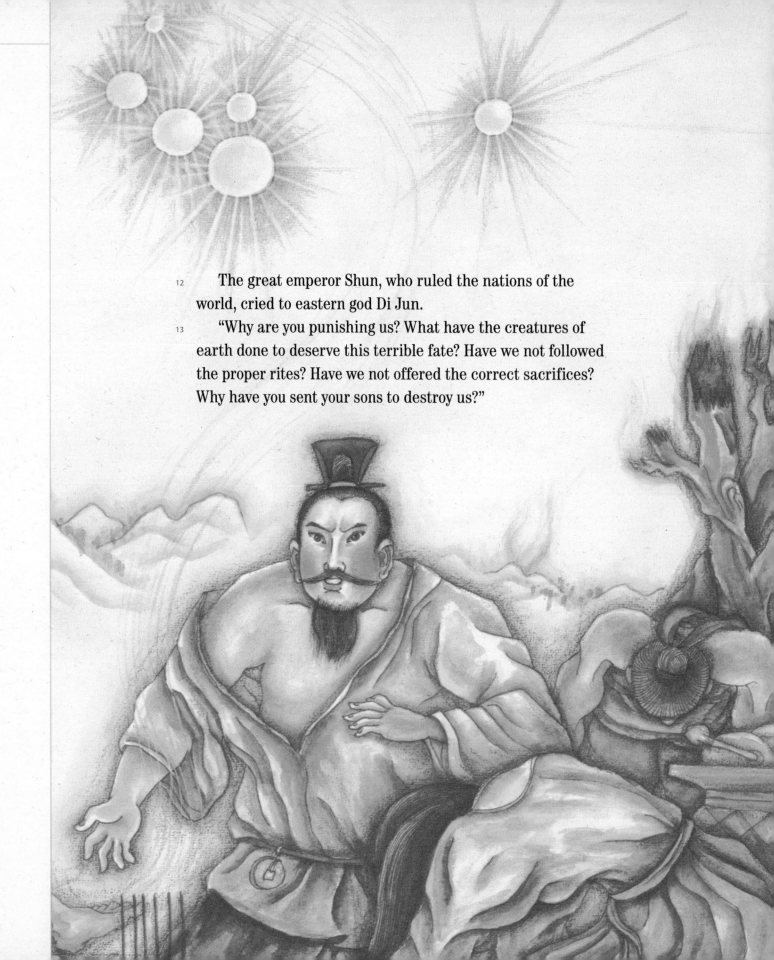

12   The great emperor Shun, who ruled the nations of the world, cried to eastern god Di Jun.

13   "Why are you punishing us? What have the creatures of earth done to deserve this terrible fate? Have we not followed the proper rites? Have we not offered the correct sacrifices? Why have you sent your sons to destroy us?"

14   The great emperor's cries woke Di Jun and Xi He. They looked out the window of the jade palace. In the distance, they saw their ten sons marching together across the sky. Di Jun and Xi He called to them, "Come back at once! Go no further!"

15   But the boys did not listen. Earth was far below. They could not see the damage they were causing. Higher and higher they climbed, until they reached the place where the sun stands at noon.

16   Di Jun could not allow the world to be destroyed. The existence of all living things depended on him. If his sons would not abandon their reckless walk, he would have to stop them. Di Jun summoned Hu Yi, the Archer of Heaven.

reckless   Someone who is reckless does not care how his or her actions affect others.

17   Hu Yi had once been a man. He introduced the science of archery to the world by inventing the bow and arrow. As a reward for his discovery, the gods placed him in the heavens among the constellations.

18   Di Jun presented Hu Yi with a magic bow and ten magic arrows. With tears filling his eyes, he told Hu Yi, "Shoot down the ten suns—my sons—who are burning up the earth."

19   Hu Yi refused. "How can I harm your boys? They are like my children. I taught them to shoot with a bow and arrow. We both still love them, even when they disobey."

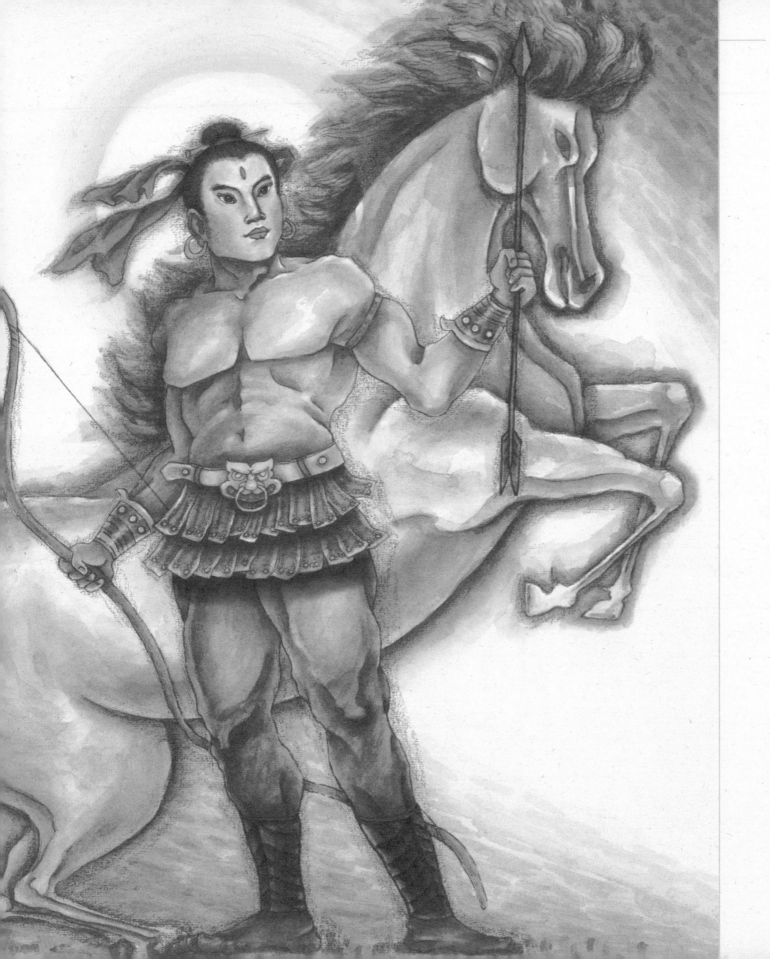

20   "I love the creatures of the earth, too. I must protect them," Di Jun told Hu Yi. "Do not be afraid. You will not harm the boys. My sons will not be hurt, but they will be changed. Never again will they cross the sky as suns. They will be gods no more. Hurry! Do as I command. There is no time to spare. The earth is dying."

21   Hu Yi took Di Jun's bow and magic arrows. He rode the wind down to earth. Taking his place on top of White Mountain, he planted his feet firmly and took careful aim.

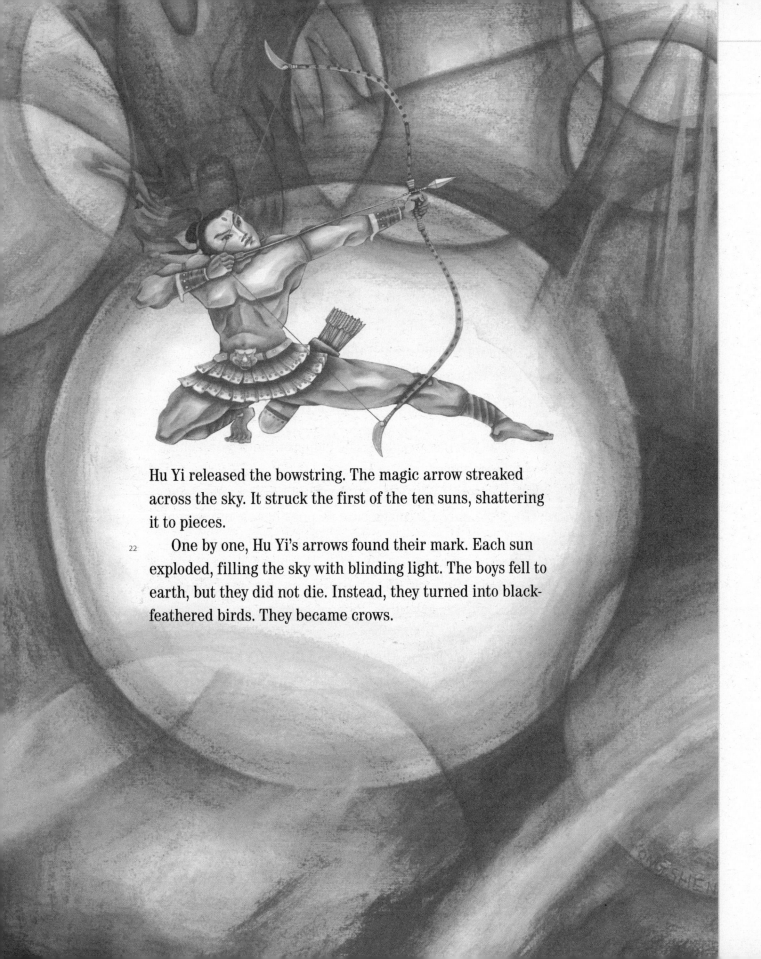

Hu Yi released the bowstring. The magic arrow streaked across the sky. It struck the first of the ten suns, shattering it to pieces.

22   One by one, Hu Yi's arrows found their mark. Each sun exploded, filling the sky with blinding light. The boys fell to earth, but they did not die. Instead, they turned into black-feathered birds. They became crows.

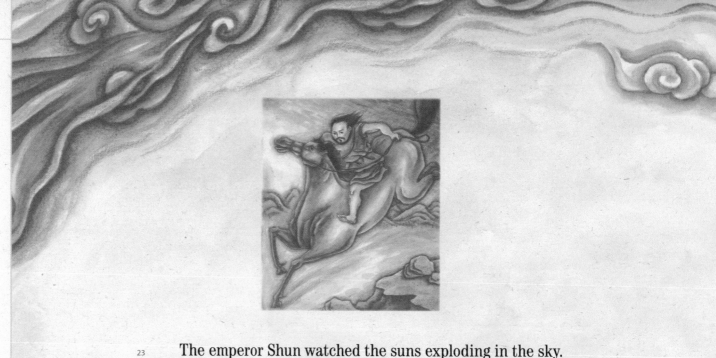

23   The emperor Shun watched the suns exploding in the sky. Suddenly he realized that if Hu Yi destroyed all the suns, there would be no heat or light. The earth would be plunged into icy darkness.

24   There was no time to spare. The emperor Shun summoned his fastest messenger.

25   "Go to the top of White Mountain. Find Hu Yi. Remove one arrow from his quiver to make sure he does not shoot down all the suns."

26   The messenger mounted his horse. He rode faster than he had ever ridden in his life, all the way to the top of White Mountain. There he saw Hu Yi. By now, only one sun remained in the sky. Shun's messenger plucked the last arrow from Hu Yi's quiver just as the Archer of Heaven reached for it. Finding no more magic arrows, Hu Yi assumed his work was done. He unstrung his bow and rode the wind back to the stars.

assumed   If you assumed something, you believed it without proof.

27   Since that day only one sun shines overhead. Every morning, the crows gather on White Mountain to greet the dawn. "*Gua! Gua!*" they call to their brother, the sun, as he begins his lonely walk across the sky.

28   For they remember that once they too were gods and hope for the day when their parents, Di Jun and Xi He, will forgive them.

The Ten Suns

As you watch *The Ten Suns,* notice how sound and images work together to tell the story. How is this story told differently from the legend you just read? How is the story supported by the images and music? Write your ideas below.

Listen for the Critical Vocabulary word *prosper*. Pay attention to clues in the images that help to explain the word's meaning. Take notes in the space below about how the word was used.

prosper   If you prosper, you succeed and do well.

Collaborative Discussion

Look back at what you wrote on page 122. Tell a partner something you learned about the text and video. Work with a group to discuss the questions below. Use details from the text and video to support your answers. Take notes for your responses.

1. Review pages 128–129. Why does the suns' decision to travel together cause problems for the people on the Earth?

2. Review pages 136–137. What problem will Earth have if the archer shoots down the ten suns? What is Di Jun's solution?

3. How is the ending in each version of the legend similar and different?

Listening Tip

Notice how each speaker uses gestures and facial expressions that help support their ideas.

Speaking Tip

When you speak, make eye contact with group members to help you know that they understand your ideas.

Write a Response

PROMPT ···

Respond to the Text and Video In *Ten Suns*, you read a Chinese legend. You also watched another version of this legend presented as a video. Think about what this legend explains about the natural world. What lessons do the characters learn? Cite evidence from the text and video to support your response.

EVIDENCE ···

List ideas from *Ten Suns* that explain ideas about the natural world. Note the lessons the characters learn.

WRITE

Now write your response in a paragraph.

Make sure your response
☐ answers the question.
☐ uses details from the legend.
☐ tells what the legend explains about the natural world.
☐ explains the lesson the characters learn.
☐ is written in complete sentences.

(?) **Essential Question**

What lessons can you learn from characters in traditional tales?

Write an Expository Essay

PROMPT Traditional tales often teach lessons. Think about the characters you read about in this module. How would you describe their traits and actions? What lessons do they learn? Write an expository essay about why it is important to consider the result of your actions. Use text evidence from at least three of the tales.

✓	Make sure your essay
☐	has an introduction.
☐	explains why people should consider the results of their actions.
☐	uses text evidence and examples from the selections.
☐	uses transitions to connect ideas.
☐	has a conclusion.

Think about the characters you read about in this module. Which of them learned a lesson? What lesson did they learn? How did they learn it? Now think about the characters you will write about. Use the chart below to plan your writing.

Characters	Characters' Traits and Actions	Events	Lesson Learned

DRAFT ·································· Write your essay.

Use the information you wrote on page 143 to draft your essay. Write a
paragraph that **introduces** the topic.

Write a **body paragraph** that describes the characters' traits and actions.
Include the lessons the characters learned. Explain what they teach readers.

Write a **conclusion** that summarizes your ideas.

The revision and editing steps give you a chance to look carefully at your writing and make changes. Work with a partner to determine whether you have explained your ideas clearly. Use these questions to help you.

✓ PURPOSE/ FOCUS	ORGANIZATION	EVIDENCE/SUPPORT	ELABORATION	CONVENTIONS
☐ Does my essay answer all the questions? ☐ Have I explained that it is important to consider the results of actions?	☐ Does my essay have a beginning and a conclusion? ☐ Did I explain my ideas in a way that makes sense?	☐ Did I use text evidence to explain how the characters learned a lesson from their actions?	☐ Have I used transitions to connect my ideas?	☐ Have I used correct punctuation and capitalization? ☐ Did I indent each new paragraph?

PUBLISH ···································· Create a finished copy.

Make a final copy of your essay. Write legibly using your cursive writing skills.

Food for Thought

"You are what
you eat."
—American saying

What can we do to make more healthful food choices?

Get Curious

Video

Five Food Groups

Examples of Healthful Foods

Healthful Food

Eco-friendly Foods

myNotes

Short Read

To Your Health!

1 Good **nutrition** is one of the keys to good health. When you eat right, your body **digests**, or breaks down, vitamins, minerals, and other nutrients that help you grow strong and stay well.

Healthy You, Healthy Planet

2 Eating well can help the planet as well as your body. When you shop with your family, look for **sustainable** foods, which are often natural, locally grown foods such as fruits and vegetables.

3 Some people **compost** bits of unused fruits, vegetables, and other natural waste. The compost can be used in their home gardens. Many cities also collect food waste to create compost. That's good news!

ChooseMyPlate.gov

Serve It Up

9 There are five food groups: protein, grains, vegetables, fruit, and dairy. According to the United States Department of Agriculture (USDA), we should aim to eat from each group every day. Here's what the USDA recommends daily for kids between ages 9 and 13.

10 **Fruits** and **vegetables** keep your heart healthy and protect you from diseases.

Daily Serving:
1½ cups of fruit and 2 to 2½ cups of vegetables

11 **Oils** are not a food group, but they provide important nutrients.

Daily Serving:
The USDA does not recommend more than 5 teaspoons of oil a day

4 Nutrition labels help you make good food choices, but they can seem mysterious. In fact, reading them can be a downright tricky. This diagram tries to take out the mystery.

5 The list of numbers on the right shows what percentage of the USDA recommended daily allowance for adults one serving contains. How many servings of this food would get you a full day's worth of the recommended fat?

Nutrition Facts

8 servings per container
Serving size   1 cup (68g)

Amount per serving
Calories   370

	% Daily Value*
Total Fat 5g	**7%**
Saturated Fat 1g	**5%**
Trans Fat 0g	
Cholesterol 0mg	**0%**
Sodium 150mg	**6%**
Total Carbohydrate 48g	**15%**
Dietary Fiber 5g	**14%**
Total Sugars 13g	
Includes 10g Added Sugars	**20%**
Protein 12g	
Vitamin A 10mcg	20%
Vitamin C 1mg	100%
Vitamin D 1mcg	50%
Vitamin E 2mcg	100%
Riboflavin 5mcg	75%
Folic Acid 200mcg	60%
Thiamin 2mcg	35%
Vitamin B12 5mcg	100%
Zinc 7mg	50%
Biotin 300mcg	100%
Calcium 50mcg	25%
Phosphorus 90mcg	90%
Magnesium 400mcg	100%
Chromium 75mcg	80%
Potassium 5g	100%

* The % Daily Value (DV) tells you how much a nutrient in a serving of food contributes to a daily diet. 2,000 calories a day is used for general nutrition advice.

6 Calories measure the energy food provides. Here, the label is telling you that 1 cup contains 370 calories.

7 Your body doesn't need added sugar, so look for foods with lower amounts.

8 Your body needs these nutrients. Look for food with high amounts. This food provides 25 percent of the calcium you need each day. How many servings of it would give you a full day's worth?

12 **Protein** is found in meat, fish, beans, eggs, nuts, and seeds. Protein helps build healthy bones, muscles, skin, and blood.

Daily Serving:
5 ounces of protein each day (1 ounce equals ¼ cup of ground meat, one egg, or a tablespoon of peanut butter.)

13 **Dairy**, such as milk, cheese, and yogurt, contains calcium and other minerals. These nutrients support strong teeth and bones.

Daily Serving:
3 cups of dairy each day (1 cup is equivalent to 1½ ounces of cheese or an 8-ounce container of yogurt.)

14 **Whole grains**, such as whole-wheat flour, oatmeal, and brown rice, help your body create energy and supply it with certain vitamins and nutrients.

Daily Serving:
5 to 6 ounces of grains each day (1 ounce equals one slice of bread or ½ cup of cooked rice, pasta, or cereal.)

Notice & Note
Contrasts and Contradictions

Prepare to Read

GENRE STUDY **Informational texts** give facts and examples about a topic.

- Authors of informational texts may organize their ideas by stating a problem and explaining its solution.
- Informational texts may include visuals, such as charts, diagrams, graphs, timelines, and maps.
- Science texts may include directions or experiments. They are organized as a series of numbered steps.

SET A PURPOSE **Think about** the title and genre of this selection. What do you know about being eco-friendly? What are some things you would like to learn about this topic? Write your ideas below.

**Build Background:
Healthful Food**

CRITICAL VOCABULARY

assess

disposable

convenient

transported

hydrated

impact

intensive

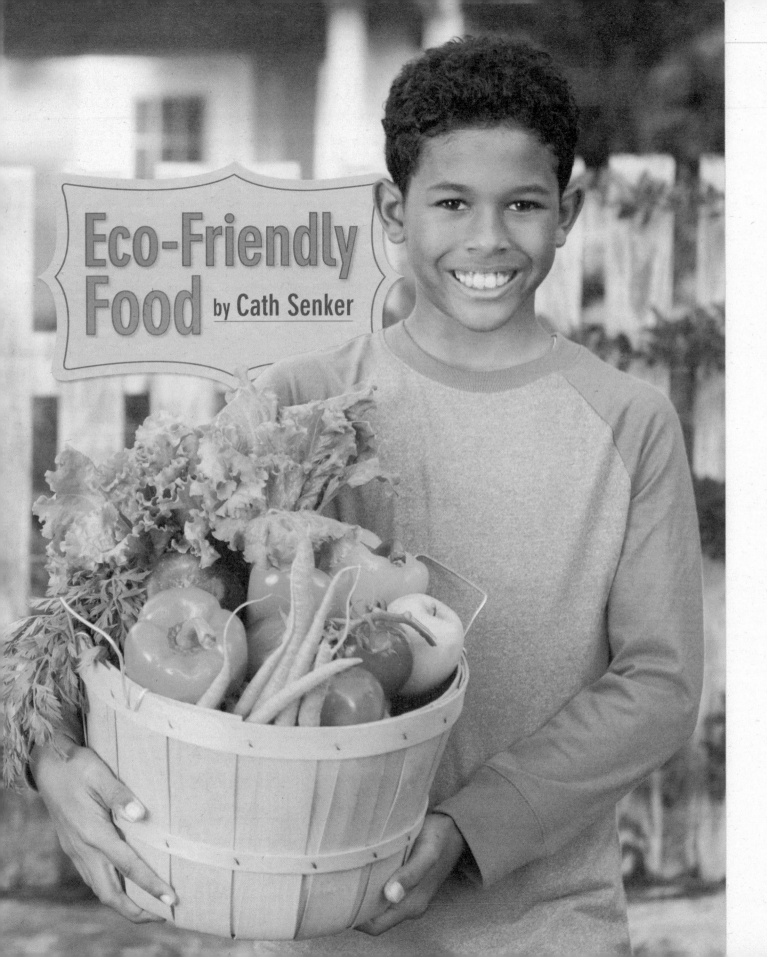

Eco-Friendly Food by Cath Senker

Are You
Wasteful
or
Waste-aware?

1 What fast and simple changes can you make so your food and drinks are more eco-friendly, cheaper, and better for you? First, **assess** yourself! Are you wasteful or waste-aware? Check this list of **disposable** items to see how your packed lunch measures up:

- sandwich in a cardboard or plastic box
- salad in a plastic box
- chips, bars, or cookies in plastic packaging

- containers of yogurt
- carton or bottle of a drink
- plastic cutlery
- plastic bags

2 If you have lots of disposable items in your lunch, consider the ideas below. Or if you're having pasta or rice for dinner, why not make a little extra to keep for lunch the next day?

1. Pick a carbohydrate (bread, pasta, rice).

2. Choose fresh vegetables in season or canned vegetables.

3. Add protein (prepared meat, canned fish, cheese, cooked beans).

4. Pack or chop fruit into natural yogurt (from a large carton).

5. Put your meal and yogurt into food containers.

6. Pour juice or water into a drink bottle (strong plastic or metal).

assess   If you assess something, you think about it carefully and judge it.

disposable   If something is disposable, it is meant to be thrown away once it has been used.

Eco Snacks

3   Of course, it can be hard to be organized enough to prepare food every day. At Ithaca Creek State Primary School, in Australia, workers at an on-site snack bar prepare sandwiches and salads with fresh ingredients—some of the produce comes from the school garden. They minimize food waste by making meals or sandwiches when they are ordered. Any leftover food goes in the compost along with fruit and vegetable peelings. The liquid from the compost fertilizes the garden, and the whole cycle begins again!

Processed Organic Foods

4   Pre-packaged organic meals and snacks are **convenient**, but are they better for the environment?

Pros

5   The ingredients are products of organic farming, which does not use chemical fertilizers that can harm wildlife.

Cons

6   Processing food requires a large amount of energy. Once produced, processed foods are packaged, **transported**, and often chilled in a refrigerator just like non-organic foods.

convenient   If something is convenient, it is handy and useful.
transported   If something is transported, it is taken from one place to another.

Think
About Your
Drink

7 There is nothing wrong with buying a soda or fruit drink every now and then when you're out. However, although some bottled drinks are healthy, many contain a large amount of sugar and additives, and they are not cheap. Also, packaging, transporting, and refrigerating the beverages come at a cost to the environment.

8 So, how can you cut down on costs and waste but stay **hydrated** and healthy? If you live in an economically developed country such as the United States, your home will have a fresh water supply—and it is probably cleaner and safer than bottled water. In some areas, the water is safe but does not taste good. You could talk to your family about buying a water filter to make tap water taste better.

hydrated Something that is hydrated has taken in plenty of water.
impact Impact is the effect that one thing has on something else.

Eco Impact

9 A U.S. report in 2010 showed that:

💧 About 50 percent of bottled water is actually tap water in a plastic bottle.

TAP

💧 About 75 percent of the bottles are thrown away, not recycled.

💧 The plastic in some bottles leaches (leaks) a substance called phthalate into the water. Some studies have linked this chemical with hormonal problems in people.

💧 Bottled water goes through fewer safety tests than tap water.

💧 Bottled water costs 100 times as much as tap water! Bottled water typically costs just over $1 for 1 gallon (3.8 liters) and much more when you buy smaller bottles. Tap water costs about 1 cent per gallon.

Growing Food

10 There is a cheap and easy way to grow food at school—even if there are no flower beds! Cylinder gardening uses containers that can be placed almost anywhere. You don't need any gardening experience, and the preparation is simple. Why not give it a try?

Make a Cylinder Garden

11 **You will need:**

- At least one 5-gallon (23-liter) bucket of the type used to transport food (you could ask a local restaurant to supply clean buckets)

- Potting soil

- Vegetable seeds

- Fertilizer

Directions

12

1 Figure out where to place your cylinder garden. You can position it on top of soil or on a human-made surface, such as concrete. Try to find an area that will receive at least six to eight hours of sunlight and is close to a source of water.

2 Research vegetables that will grow during the season you are in. If you are gardening at school, look for varieties that you can harvest within a school quarter or semester—30 to 90 days. Search for compact varieties that can grow in a small space. The vegetables that are suitable for cylinder gardening are beans, carrots, parsley, peas, or tomatoes.

3 Cut off the bottom of the bucket and discard it. Then cut the rest of the bucket in half. You will need to ask an adult to help you. Now you have two cylinders. (Note: If you are placing the bucket on concrete, it is better not to cut it, but ask an adult to drill drainage holes in the bottom.)

4 Put the cylinders in position.

5 Fill them with potting soil and mix in some fertilizer.

6 Plant your seeds, following the instructions on the package for spacing, and water gently.

7 Monitor the seedlings as they grow, keeping them moist with water and adding fertilizer regularly. Thin out the seedlings if they are crushed together.

159

Food Miles

13 Growing your own vegetables reduces food miles. The principle behind food miles is that the farther away your food is produced, the worse for the environment. However, keep in mind that beans that are produced locally using oil-based fertilizers and plowed by diesel tractors could be worse than beans grown by less energy-**intensive** methods in another country. Storing local food for a long time to be eaten out of season can also use up a lot of energy.

Being Green: Summing Up

14 • **Make eco-friendly packed meals and snacks.**

• **Stay hydrated by drinking tap water.**

• **Grow your own food.**

---

intensive   Something that is intensive uses a lot of effort to complete a task.

Collaborative Discussion

Look back at what you wrote on page 152. Tell a partner two things you learned from this text. Then work with a group to discuss the questions below. Support your ideas with information and details from *Eco-Friendly Food*. Take notes for your responses. When you speak, use your notes.

1 Review page 154. Which of the ideas that the author lists are wasteful? Which are waste-aware?

2 Reread page 158. What reasons does the author give for making a cylinder garden?

3 What are some ways that growing food at a school garden can be useful?

Listening Tip

As you listen to each speaker's ideas, think about how you can connect your own ideas to them.

Speaking Tip

Make sure you use eye contact when you state your ideas and supported opinions.

Write a Response

PROMPT ....

Respond to the Text In *Eco-Friendly Food,* you read about some ways to make environmentally friendly and healthful food choices. What are some of these choices? What kinds of eco-friendly food choices can you make every day? Cite evidence from the text to support your response. Try to use Critical Vocabulary words in your response.

EVIDENCE ....

List ideas from *Eco-Friendly Food* that tell how to make healthful and eco-friendly food choices.

WRITE ....

Now write your response in a paragraph.

✓	**Make sure your response**
☐	answers the questions.
☐	uses evidence from the text.
☐	describes healthful food choices.
☐	explains eco-friendly food choices.
☐	is written in complete sentences.

Prepare to View

GENRE STUDY **Recipe videos** show the steps to complete a recipe in a visual and audio format.

- A narrator introduces the ingredients needed to complete the recipe.
- A narrator explains and shows viewers the steps to complete a recipe.
- Recipe videos might include text on the screen to show ingredients and describe the steps for cooking.

SET A PURPOSE **As you watch**, think about what you know about cooking healthful meals. What are some things about nutritious meals that you would like to learn? Write your ideas below.

CRITICAL VOCABULARY

adventurous

unique

Build Background: Cooking

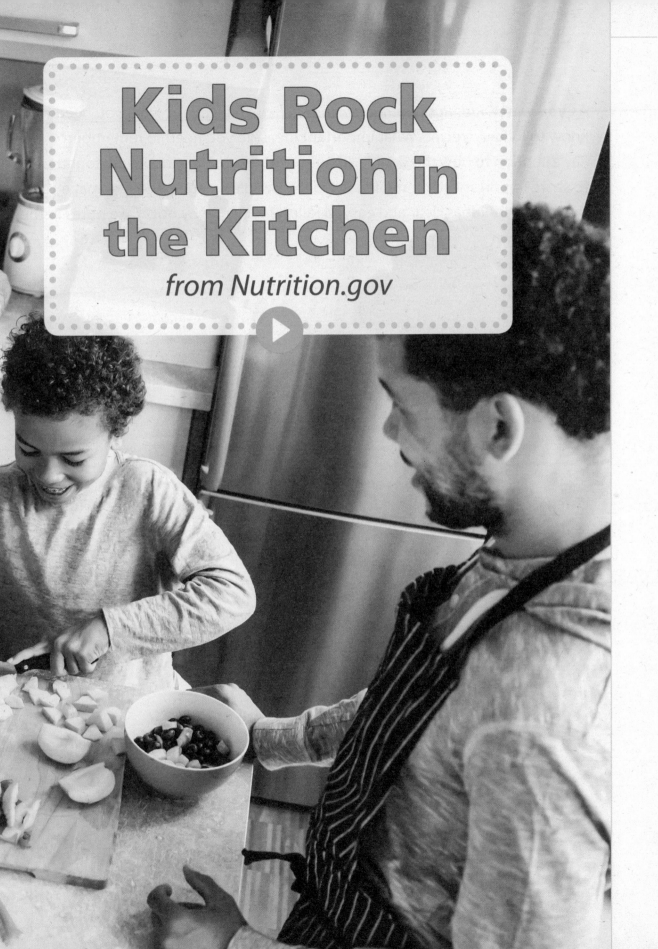

Kids Rock Nutrition in the Kitchen

from Nutrition.gov

As you watch *Kids Rock Nutrition in the Kitchen*, think about what you need to know to follow a recipe. What important ideas do you need to remember? Pay attention to how the people, images, and text in the video work together to share important steps and ideas. Do the people, images, and text make the important ideas clear and easy to follow? Why or why not? Take notes in the space below.

Listen for the Critical Vocabulary words *adventurous* and *unique*. Listen for clues to the meaning of each word.

adventurous   Someone who is adventurous tries to do new things.
unique   Something that is unique is different or one of a kind.

Collaborative Discussion

Look back on what you wrote on page 164. Tell a partner two things you learned from this video. Then discuss the questions below. Refer to the details in the video to support your ideas. Take notes for your responses. When you speak, use your notes.

1 What does the dietitian suggest about how to prepare a fish or chicken packet?

2 What do the students learn about the steps for making a fruit parfait?

3 Review the video segment from 01:00 to 01:15. What key points about chicken and fish does the dietitian share?

Listening Tip

Show you are paying attention by looking at your partner as he or she shares their ideas. Make note of any ideas you want to know more about.

Speaking Tip

After you speak, ask your partner to share his or her questions or comments about what you have said.

Write a Response

PROMPT ....

Respond to the Video In *Kids Rock Nutrition in the Kitchen,* you learned how to make a tasty and nutritious meal. Think about the healthful meal the dietitian made with the students. What types of foods were used? What foods were recommended as healthy choices to use in a meal? Cite evidence from the video to support your response.

EVIDENCE ....

List ideas from *Kids Rock Nutrition in the Kitchen* that tell how to make healthful food choices when preparing a meal.

WRITE

Now write your response in a paragraph.

✓	**Make sure your response**

☐	answers the questions.
☐	uses evidence from the video.
☐	explains some healthful food choices.
☐	tells how to make healthful food choices when preparing a meal.
☐	is written in complete sentences.

Prepare to Read

GENRE STUDY **Informational texts** give facts and examples about a topic.

- Authors of informational texts may organize their ideas using headings and subheadings.
- Authors of informational texts may also organize ideas by comparing and contrasting.
- Informational texts may include text features, such as bold print, captions, and italics.

SET A PURPOSE **Think about** the title and genre of this text. What do you know about the unusual foods people in other countries eat? What would you like to learn? Write your ideas below.

Build Background: Unusual Foods

CRITICAL VOCABULARY

pests

edible

forbidden

attitudes

BUG BITES

1   *Have you heard the one about the customer who finds a fly in his soup? Outraged, he points it out to the waiter, who says, "Keep your voice down, or everybody'll want one!" OK, so it's an old joke. But the funny part is what the waiter says. Who on earth would want to eat a bug?*

2   Well, would it surprise you if we said lots of people would? It's true. In Australia, South America, Africa, and Asia, eating bugs is no joke. Bugs aren't just pests. They're lunch or dinner or a nice afterschool snack.

3   To those of us who've never crunched a cricket or slurped a worm, the idea of eating bugs sounds pretty gross. We wouldn't eat those creepy-crawlies even if someone dared us! Yet lots of bugs are nutritious, tasty, and perfectly safe to eat.

| pests | Pests are insects or small animals that harm crops or annoy people. |

EAT UP! WE'RE OUTNUMBERED

4 Eating bugs is an old habit. Ten thousand years ago, before they learned to farm, our ancestors found food by hunting and gathering. Bugs were considered part of the daily diet. It made sense for ancient people to eat a source of nutrition that was right under their noses—or buzzing by their ears.

5 As you've probably noticed, bugs are everywhere. One out of every three animals is a bug, and scientists estimate that there are 200 million of the little critters for every person on the planet. No wonder more than half the people on earth still eat bugs daily. Of the million or so types of bug that scientists have named so far, more than 1,500 are somebody's favorite snack.

6 The most popular bugs to eat are crickets and termites, which are said to taste a bit like pineapple, but lots of other bugs are edible, too. Restaurants in Mexico sell ant tacos. Cans of baby bees line supermarket shelves in Japan. In Thailand, outdoor markets offer silkworm larvae. And in Mozambique, in eastern Africa, people call grasshoppers "flying shrimp."

> **edible** If something is edible, it is safe for people to eat.

In the United States, a candy company sells bug-filled lollipops.

This clay pan is filled with dried grasshopper snacks. You can find these snacks all over Mexico.

173

Which is more nutritious—
ground beef or grasshoppers?
▼

At this market in Thailand,
people can buy a variety of
fried insects.
▼

BUGS DO A BODY GOOD

7   Dinner is served: on one plate, a big, juicy hamburger, and on the other, a heaping pile of cooked grasshoppers. Ground beef or bugs? Which one do you think is better for your body?

8   Both have lots of protein, which is what your body uses to build muscle. But in other ways, grasshoppers clearly come out ahead. A pound of grasshoppers has less fat than a pound of beef, and the insects are higher in calcium and iron. Other bugs are good for you, too. Says biologist David George Gordon, author of the Eat-a-Bug Cookbook, "I tell kids, if your bones are still growing, eat more crickets and termites."

9   Still wouldn't pick the grasshoppers? Gordon says they also taste delicious, a lot like green peppers.

A MATTER OF TASTE

10   In North America and Europe, the idea of eating bugs is downright disgusting to most people. But even though we don't think of crickets and termites as food, lots of things we do eat are bug-related. Honey is made by bees. Shrimp, crayfish, crabs, and lobsters are all arthropods, which is what scientists call the bug group of animals. In fact, lobsters have only recently made the transition from bug to edible treat. The first American colonists ate lobsters only when they didn't have anything else. In Massachusetts, servants who were tired of getting the "cockroaches of the sea" for dinner wrote into their contracts that they'd eat lobster only three times a week.

They may look scary, but these fried scorpion kebabs are a popular snack in China.

11   Other parts of the world also have forbidden foods. Lots of people would never eat lobsters and the other sea-dwelling "bugs" we consider delicacies. Many people don't eat pork. Even among people who eat insects, tastes differ. South Africans might munch termites for lunch, but they'd never eat scorpions, which are raised for food in China. In Bali, Indonesia, dragonflies are a treat, but in the Indonesian province of Irian Jaya, no one would think of eating a dragonfly. Cicadas are on the menu instead.

12   So when it comes to eating, people mostly stick with food they're used to. What's food and what's not is a matter of taste—and what you've been taught.

forbidden   If something is forbidden, it is not allowed or accepted.

FUTURE FOOD

13 Could our tastes change? Could school lunches ever include grasshopper kabobs and caterpillar fritters?

14 Attitudes about bugs are already changing. Thanks to bug-appreciation programs at schools and science centers, kids today are less squeamish about insects. If we can get over the "Gross!" factor, bugs could one day become part of our daily diet. Bugs are even considered a perfect food for long space journeys, because astronauts could breed them in outer space.

15 Still wondering who on earth would want to eat a bug? Better to ask, who wouldn't?

> **attitudes**   Your attitudes are the ways you think and feel about something.

This fried insect burger may look unusual, but it's a popular meal in some countries.

BUG BITES

Collaborative Discussion

Look back at what you wrote on page 170. Tell a partner two things you learned from this text. Work with a group to discuss the questions below. Support your ideas with details from *Bug Bites*. Take notes for your responses. When you speak, use your notes.

1 Review page 172. Which words reveal the author's perspective on eating bugs?

> THer're lunch or dinner or a nice afternoon snack.

2 Reread pages 173–174. What examples does the author provide to support the popularity of eating bugs?

> more than 1,500 Bugs are someones favorite snack.

3 How does the author use humor to make the ideas in the selection convincing?

>

Listening Tip

Be an active listener! Focus on what each person is saying. Try jotting down a few notes to help you remember important points.

Speaking Tip

Be sure to use the correct rate and volume when you state and support your opinions. Be sure to speak clearly.

Write a Response

PROMPT

Respond to the Text In *Bug Bites,* you learned about some of the bugs that people around the world like to eat as part of a healthful diet. Think about the types of bugs you read about. What are the advantages of eating the bugs discussed in the text? How can these bugs be considered part of a healthful diet? Cite evidence from the text to support your response.

EVIDENCE

List ideas from *Bug Bites* that tell how some bugs can be part of a healthful diet.

WRITE ....

Now write your response in a paragraph.

✓

Make sure your response

☐	answers the questions.
☐	uses evidence from the text.
☐	explains the benefits of eating bugs.
☐	tells how some bugs can be part of a healthful diet.
☐	is written in complete sentences.

Notice & Note
Words of the Wiser

Prepare to Read

GENRE STUDY **Realistic fiction** tells a story about characters and events that are like those in real life.

- Realistic fiction includes characters who act, think, and speak like real people.
- Realistic fiction includes dialogue to develop the story.
- Authors of realistic fiction may tell the story through third-person point of view. In third-person point of view, the story is told through an outside observer.

SET A PURPOSE **Look at** the title and picture on the next page. What do you think the girl is getting ready to do? Write your ideas below.

**Meet the Author:
René Saldaña, Jr.**

CRITICAL VOCABULARY

react

astounded

luscious

culinary

offense

crestfallen

opted

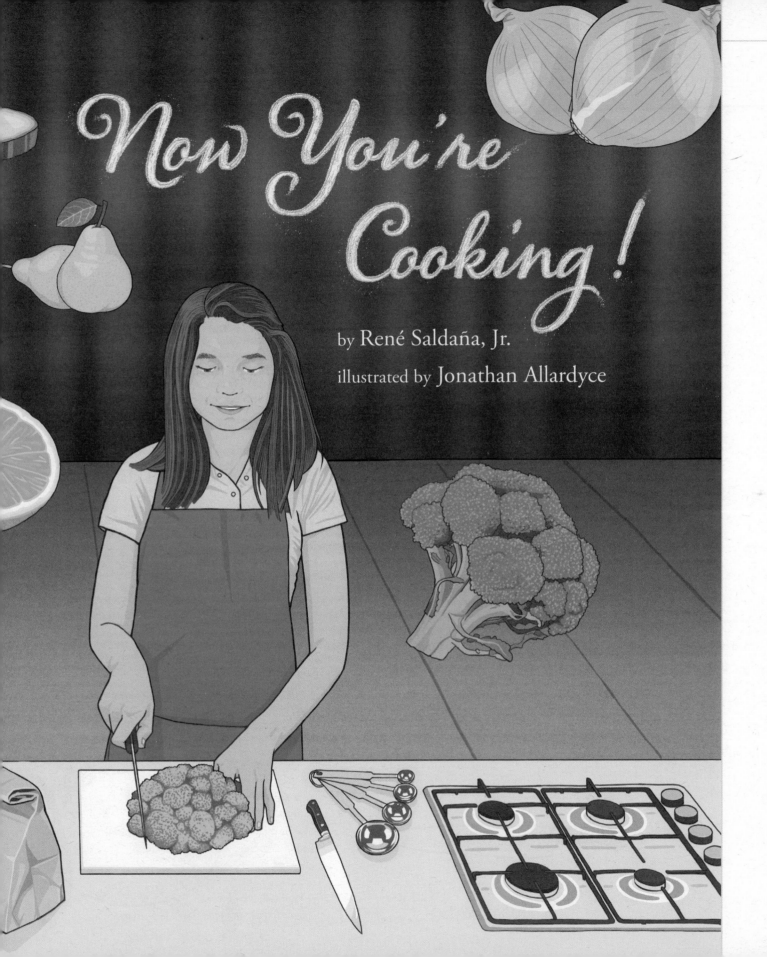

Now You're Cooking!

by René Saldaña, Jr.

illustrated by Jonathan Allardyce

1   Martina Deanda couldn't have been more nervous. A few moments ago she had heard her name announced on the school intercom. She was one of two finalists in the Spring Cook-Off, an annual event sponsored by the school district and the local farmers market. She couldn't believe that she'd made it this far. Before she'd entered the contest, her experience in the kitchen had been limited to pouring milk on her cereal for breakfast. Otherwise, her cooking skills were nonexistent. She was an avid viewer of television cooking shows, though.

2   Her best friend, Avani, came up to her smiling, hugged her, and said, "Now you're cooking!" Avani chuckled at her own pun. When Martina didn't react, Avani said, "Get it? You're in a cooking competition and you're moving on to the final cook-off, so now you're cooking? Right?"

react   When you react to something, you act in a way that shows you are aware of it.

3   It wasn't that she didn't get it. Martina was just astounded that she'd made it to the finals. She was competing with her classmate Joey Cardenas, whose mother owned the best Mexican restaurant in town, La Tampiqueña. On weekends, Joey helped in the restaurant bussing tables, sweeping the floors, and learning to cook from the chef on Saturdays between lunch and dinner service. He was sure to win.

4   Martina wished she could share in Avani's excitement. "More like my goose is cooked," she told her friend.

5   "You won't win with that kind of attitude," said Avani. "You should be more positive."

6   "Why? I mean, Joey knows how to cook. Me? I only have my cooking shows for inspiration."

7   Avani put her hands on Martina's shoulders. "You're just looking at this all wrong. You don't know as much about cooking as Joey does, but look how far you've gotten today. There were ten contestants. First, you baked some luscious breakfast empanadas, and then you made that roasted vegetable panini that the judges described as "mouth-watering." Now the competition is down to the two best cooks—you and Joey. That should tell you *some*thing."

> **astounded**   If you are astounded by something, you are completely surprised by it.
> **luscious**   A food that is luscious is tasty and often juicy.

myNotes

8   "I guess you're right. I'm just nervous."

9   Avani smiled. "I think most people are nervous when they compete. It means what you are doing is really important to you."

10   "It really is," Martina said. "Thanks, Avani."

11   Moments later, a voice on the intercom asked for everyone but the two contestants to leave the stage. "Contestants, it's time for you to show off your culinary skills," announced emcee and local television news anchor Jack Jackson. Joey Cardenas's mom whispered some last-second advice in his ear and left the stage.

12   Joey looked confident as he walked up to the girls. "You ready, Freddy?" he asked.

13   "Hey, Joey," said Avani, "Martina is more than ready." As she turned to go Avani looked over her shoulder and said, "She's so on fire today that the thermometer's going to explode!"

culinary Something that is culinary is connected to cooking.

185

14   Joey chuckled for a moment, but then his expression became serious. "You ready for this?" he asked Martina.

15   "As much as I'll ever be. You?"

16   "Well, you know, cooking's in my genes," he said. "No offense."

17   "None taken," she responded. "But don't be surprised if I cook circles around you."

18   "If you say so. May the best cook win!" With that, the two took their places.

19   Mr. Jackson joined them at the table where two paper bags from the farmers market awaited them. The audience became quiet. Mr. Jackson looked out over the crowd and said, "We have come to my favorite part of this competition, the finale." In addition to being the emcee, Mr. Jackson had served as one of the judges for the very first Spring Cook-Off ever. Mrs. Cardenas, Joey's mom, had won that one.

> **offense**   An offense is something that makes you feel hurt, annoyed, or insulted.

myNotes

20   Martina looked over at Joey, who, for the first time since the start of the competition, looked nervous. He kept fidgeting with the strings on his apron. Martina imagined that the Cardenas family reputation was on the line.

21   Martina looked out at the audience and saw her own parents, both beaming with pride. Avani was sitting next to them, pumping a fist in the air and mouthing the words, "Go, Martina!"

22   Mr. Jackson asked the contestants to empty their bags. "Carefully, though. You don't want to crack those eggs. Your challenge is this: using part or all of every ingredient in the bag, plus a dash of this or a pinch of that, make a delicious, healthful meal."

23   In each bag there were three eggs, a red and a yellow bell pepper, a tomato, strawberries, and a peach. A rack of spices, seasonings, and other ingredients stood next to the table. Martina looked over at Joey, who was now smiling, rubbing his hands together. She could almost see the gears turning in his brain. He knew what he was making. She had no clue.

24   "You'll have 20 minutes," said Mr. Jackson. "Cooks, are you ready?" The two nodded. Joey was anxious to get to work. Martina was still thinking, but wasn't coming up with anything. *Oh, no,* she thought, *Joey's going to win this competition!*

25   "Cook!" cried Mr. Jackson and started the timer.

26   Martina ran over to the rack to see if looking at all the spices and other ingredients would inspire her. She saw a basket of bread. Sitting on top were two *bolillos* (boh-LEE-yohz), a kind of bread that reminded her of early mornings visiting her grandparents in Mexico—warm, toasty mornings.

27   Then it struck her. She had more than just the cooking shows to inspire her! She also had memories of her abuelito Servando teaching her to fix his favorite breakfast. Martina took the two pieces of bread, a sprig of cilantro, and some butter, and then she got cooking.

* * *

28   In the end, Martina didn't win the cook-off, but she wasn't crestfallen. She noticed that the judges had finished all of her dish, while Joey's was left half-eaten. Mr. Jackson reminded her that the instructions called for a healthful meal, and though she had used the peppers, tomato, strawberries, and peach, she still could've separated the egg whites from the yolks and opted for olive oil instead of butter. "But I'll tell you what, Ms. Deanda," he said, "that was one delicious meal."

29   Martina walked up to Joey, who held the trophy over his head. "Congratulations, Joey," she said. "You cooked a better meal than mine."

30   "It looks that way," he said. But he glanced at the judges' plates. "There's always next year, though."

31   *Yes,* she thought. *There's always next year.* And there would be many more visits to her grandparents' home between now and then. She couldn't wait for her next visit! Maybe she'd give them a telephone call that night and tell them about the competition.

> **crestfallen**   If you are crestfallen, you are sad and discouraged.
> **opted**   If you opted for something, you chose it.

Bolillo Boats

Ingredients

- 2 bolillos or other soft white rolls
- 1 tablespoon butter, melted
- 2 eggs
- 1 tablespoon butter or olive oil (for cooking the eggs)
- ¼ cup shredded Monterey Jack cheese
- 2 slices of tomato
- 2 slices of red, yellow, or orange bell pepper
- a few sprigs of cilantro

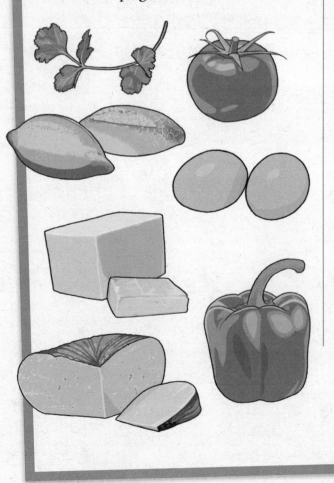

Instructions

Have an adult help you when using the stove and oven.

1. Preheat oven to 350º.
2. Gently pinch out the middle of the bolillos. They should look like little bread boats.
3. Brush the melted butter onto each bolillo, inside and out.
4. Place bolillos on a baking sheet and bake for 5 minutes. Once lightly toasted, remove from oven.
5. While bread is baking, fry the two eggs and slices of pepper in butter or olive oil. Try cracking the egg inside the slice of pepper.
6. Spoon a fried egg and a slice of pepper into each of the bread boats and top with a slice of tomato. Sprinkle cheese evenly onto the bread boats and bake for another 5–10 minutes or until cheese has melted.
7. Ask an adult to remove the baking sheet from the hot oven. Garnish with a sprig of cilantro. Serve with sliced peaches and strawberries on the side.

Collaborative Discussion

Look back at what you wrote on page 180. Tell a partner two things you learned about the main character, Martina. Then work with a group to discuss the questions below. Find support for your answers in *Now You're Cooking!* During the discussion, ask questions to find out more about others' ideas.

1 Review pages 183–184. What details in the text show how Martina feels about being in the finals?

2 Review page 189. How does Martina feel about the results of the cook-off? How do you know?

3 What parts of the story are presented in a realistic way? Explain your thinking.

Listening Tip

Listen carefully to identify each speaker's key ideas. What questions can you ask to find out about these ideas?

Speaking Tip

Speak in complete sentences and use correct grammar to clearly express your ideas and supported opinions.

Write a Response

PROMPT ....

Respond to the Text In *Now You're Cooking!,* you read about a girl in a cooking competition. Think about the task that the contestants are given. What knowledge does Martina need to win the contest? Why is she concerned about her competitor? Cite evidence from the text to support your response.

EVIDENCE ....

List ideas from *Now You're Cooking!* that tell about the cooking competition and why Martina is concerned about her competitor.

Now write your response in a paragraph.

Make sure your response

- [ ] answers the questions.
- [ ] uses evidence from the text.
- [ ] explains the task given to the contestants.
- [ ] tells why Martina is worried about her competitor.
- [ ] is written in complete sentences.

Essential Question

What can we do to make more healthful food choices?

Write an Opinion Essay

PROMPT Think about what you learned from the selections in this module about healthful food choices.

Why should people make more healthful food choices? What types of foods make up a healthful diet? Use evidence from the selections to write an opinion essay that tells why it is important to eat nutritious foods and to avoid sugary, high-fat foods.

Make sure your opinion essay
☐ states your opinion clearly in an introduction.
☐ is organized into paragraphs that give reasons that support your opinion.
☐ includes evidence from the texts and video.
☐ uses persuasive language.
☐ ends with a conclusion that will leave readers with something to think about.

What are some changes you can make every day for better health? What evidence from the texts and video supports your opinion? Use the chart below to plan your writing.

Healthful Changes	Evidence from the Texts and Video

DRAFT ·· Write your opinion essay.

Use the information you wrote on page 195 to draft your opinion essay. Write an **introduction** that states your opinion.

[ ]

↓

Write a **body paragraph** that includes reasons for your opinion. Cite text evidence that supports each reason. Use transitions to connect your ideas.

[ ]

↓

Write a **conclusion** that restates your opinion and summarizes your ideas.

[ ]

REVISE AND EDIT

Review your draft.

The revision and editing steps give you a chance to look carefully at your draft and make changes. Work with a partner to determine whether you have clearly supported your opinion and explained your ideas. Use these questions to help you.

✓ PURPOSE/ FOCUS	ORGANIZATION	EVIDENCE/SUPPORT	ELABORATION	CONVENTIONS
☐ Have I clearly stated my opinion? ☐ Did I explain why it's important to eat more nutritious foods?	☐ Does my opinion have a clear introduction? ☐ Does my conclusion summarize the reasons for my opinion?	☐ Did I include evidence and examples from the selections to support my opinion?	☐ Did I use transition words to connect ideas? ☐ Did I use persuasive language?	☐ Have I used correct punctuation and capitalization? ☐ Have I spelled all the words correctly?

PUBLISH

Create a finished copy.

Make a final copy of your opinion essay. Write legibly using your cursive writing skills.

Global Guardians

"The environment is where we all meet . . . it is the one thing all of us share."

—Lady Bird Johnson

? Essential Question

What can people do to care for our planet?

Get Curious
▶
Video

Solutions

Protecting the Planet

Act Locally

Protect
Animals

ecology Ecology is the relationship between the living things in their environment.

conservation Conservation is the act of saving and protecting the environment.

sanctuary A sanctuary is where people or animals go to be safe from danger.

recycle If you recycle something, you put it through a process so that it can be reused.

 myNotes

November 19

Emelia Garcia
Vice President, Global Solutions
Active Environmental
500 Main Street
Waco, TX 76633

The Eco Guardians

Dear Ms. Garcia:

1 We are the Eco Guardians, a group of students who are passionate about ecology and conservation. Our faculty adviser, Catherine Leominster, suggested we contact you since you're an expert on environmental issues. Plus, you were her college roommate!

2 We would appreciate your advice on ways to help the environment. One of our ideas is to host an annual environmental awareness day in our town, in which residents could pick up trash in conservation areas and educate others about recycling, biking, and other ways to help the environment. Can you recommend other activities?

3 We have another idea, too. Our city has several acres of vacant land, and some people want to develop it and put up buildings. However, we think the land should become a sanctuary for birds and animals. It has a lot of trees, a pond, and some marshland, so it seems ideal for this purpose. Do you have any thoughts on how we can help make this happen?

4 We look forward to hearing from you, and thank you very much for your time!

Sincerely,

Jolena Walker
The Eco Guardians

5 P.S. Please remember to recycle this letter. It's always better to reuse things, even paper!

December 1

Eco Guardians
Peabody Elementary School
70 Ridge Avenue
Dallas, TX 02140

Dear Jolena and the Eco Guardians,

1   I'm responding to your letter about helping
the environment.

2   Let me start by saying I'm delighted the Eco Guardians
exist! Earth's future is in the hands of young people like
yourselves, and your efforts can help make a clean, green
world for generations to come.

3   An environmental awareness day sounds terrific! You might
consider planting trees or starting a community garden, or
both. People love getting their hands dirty. When they see a
sapling grow or a seed sprout, it brings them closer to nature
and makes them care about protecting it.

4   The sanctuary is also a wonderful idea. It would preserve many
animal habitats and provide a place for people to enjoy nature. I
suggest asking your parents to start a petition. If many people sign
the petition, your town may decide to set aside the land rather than
develop it. Make sure the petition describes the land's natural
features and some of the animals that live there. The more
people know, the more likely they'll be to support you.

5   Thanks so much for writing, and please let me know how
your projects go. Also, please say hello to Mrs. Leominster
for me. She was the best roommate in the world!

Sincerely,

Emelia Garcia
Vice President, Global Solutions
Active Environmental

6   P.S. I probably don't need to remind you to
recycle this letter!

Notice & Note
Tough Questions

Prepare to Read

GENRE STUDY **Graphic novels** are longer fictional stories told in comic-strip format.

- Graphic novels tell stories through speech bubbles and illustrated panels.
- Authors of graphic novels tell the story through the plot—the main events of the story.
- Graphic novels can include characters who act, think, and speak like real people.

SET A PURPOSE **Think about** the title and topic of this module. What do you think will happen to Luz? What would you like to learn about her? Write your ideas below.

Meet the Author:
Claudia Dávila

CRITICAL VOCABULARY
frequent
sufficient
oasis
permission
installing
abandoned

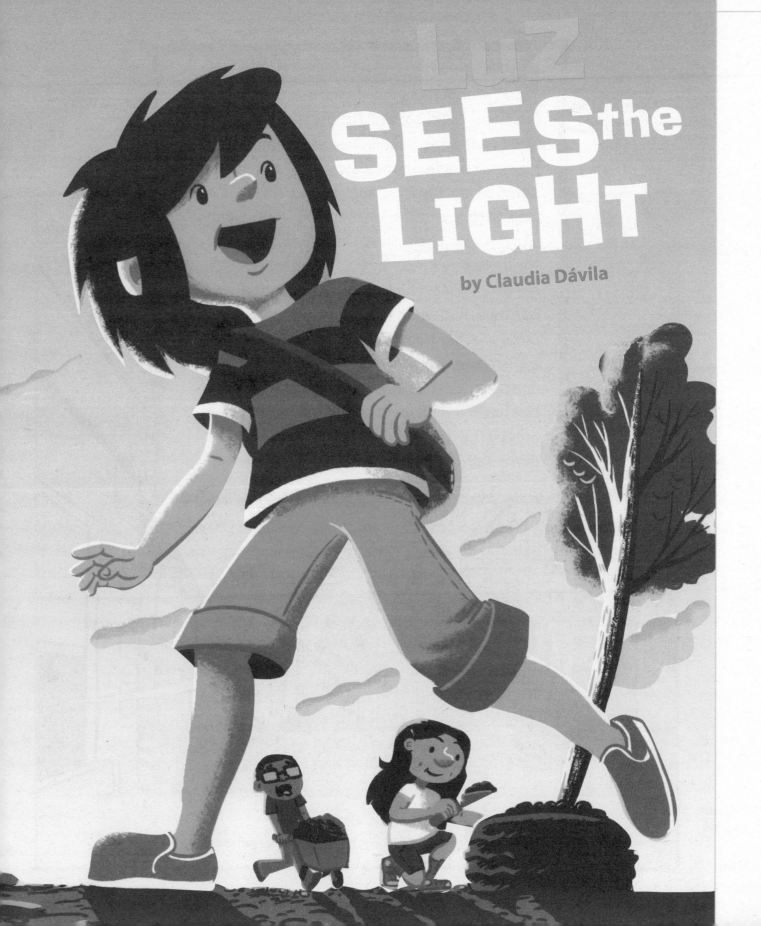

Luz SEES the LIGHT

by Claudia Dávila

Luz (pronounced *loose*) and her friends enjoy listening to music and frequent trips to the mall. Then Luz's neighborhood is dimmed by blackouts, and she realizes that she can't do some of her favorite activities. While out on a walk with her new friend Robert, her neighbor Gord warns them that they need to prepare for more blackouts by becoming more self-sufficient. Luz thinks Gord's ideas are a bit strange, but when the price of gas goes up, Luz's mother points out that it affects everything from driving to the mall to the cost of groceries and even the new sneakers Luz has been saving for. Luz realizes that maybe it's time to use less energy and be more self-sufficient.

YAWN!

frequent   If something is frequent, it happens often.
sufficient   If something is sufficient, it is just what is needed and no more.

myNotes

209

oasis   An oasis is a relaxing or peaceful spot in an area that is unpleasant in some way.

myNotes

permission If you get permission, someone who is in charge allows you to do what you asked to do.

214

myNotes

Ugh! Am I totally out to lunch? What if my idea really is crazy?

Maybe I can't turn a garbage dump into a garden. Everyone will say a farm park is a stupid idea.

It even sounds silly! Mom would say I'm totally dreaming.

But don't people see that things are changing? And that we need to change, too?

LATER THAT WEEK...

Sigh.

clik

Well, here goes nothing.

Uh, hi! Hello! How would you like to help me start a farm in the city?

I don't want to buy whatever it is you're selling!

219

Number ten-o-six?

That's us!

Maybe there's an answer from the city about getting permission to use the lot!

WINNER!

Argh! Just junk mail.

All right. That's it. If no one's going to help me, I'll turn that lot into a food park myself!

A FEW MINUTES LATER...

Okay, I got gloves and a garbage bag.

Time to take out the trash!

Here I am, trying to get my neighbors together, and no one's around—or even interested! I try to get my friends on board, and they laugh at me!

Sigh!

I can't do it by myself.

And why should I? The park is for everyone, not just for me!

LUZ!

Oh, great.

Uh, can I help you?

Au contraire!

So, like, Robert told me about what your park idea was all about, and well... it sounds like A LOT of work—

And maybe—hopefully!—there will be no real need to grow our own food!

Okay, I get it! You think it's a stupid idea!

installing If you are installing something, you are setting it up so it is ready to use.

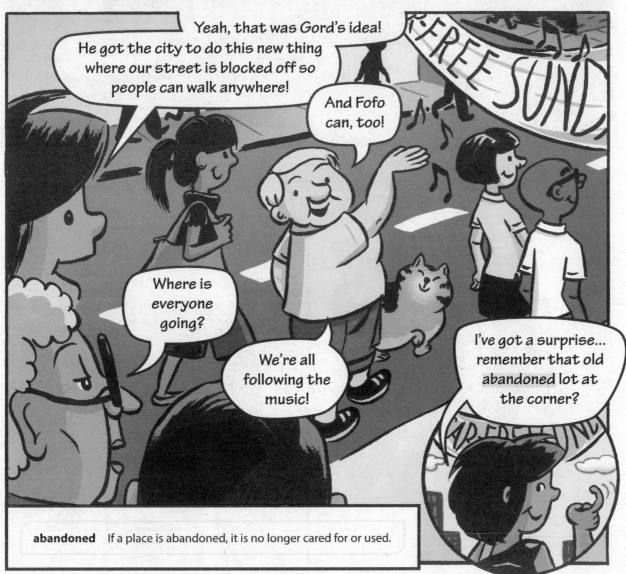

abandoned   If a place is abandoned, it is no longer cared for or used.

234

Collaborative Discussion

Look back at what you wrote on page 204. Tell a partner two things you learned from this story. Then work with a group to discuss the questions below. Refer to details in *Luz Sees the Light*. Take notes for your responses. When you speak, use your notes.

1. Reread pages 210–211. What does Luz want to do with the empty lot in her neighborhood?

2. Review pages 218–221. Why does Luz feel discouraged when she starts her project?

3. Why does Luz think her project will help the community and the planet?

Listening Tip

As you listen carefully to others, decide whether or not you agree. You can respond by saying "I agree because . . ." or by suggesting a different perspective.

Speaking Tip

Jot down a few notes from the text that will help you answer each question. Refer to your notes as you speak.

235

Write a Response

Respond to the Text In *Luz Sees the Light,* you read about a determined girl who turns an abandoned city lot into a beautiful park. Think about Luz's thoughts and actions. Why does Luz want to turn the lot into a park? How does she do her part to care for the environment? Cite evidence from the text to support your response.

List ideas from *Luz Sees the Light* that show why Luz wants to turn the abandoned lot into a park and how she shows her care for the environment.

WRITE

Now write your response in a paragraph.

✓ **Make sure your response**

☐	answers the questions.
☐	uses details from the text.
☐	explains why Luz wants to turn the lot into a park.
☐	tells how Luz shows her care for the environment.
☐	is written in complete sentences.

Notice &
Note
Tough Questions

Prepare to Read and View

GENRE STUDY **Realistic fiction** tells a story about characters and events that are like those in real life.

- Authors of realistic fiction may use figurative language to develop the setting and the characters.
- Realistic fiction includes informal language to make conversations seem real.

Saving the Kemp's Ridley Sea Turtle

Informational videos present facts and information about a topic in visual and audio form. Videos may include clips of animals in the wild to illustrate the topic.

SET A PURPOSE **Think about** the title and genre of this text and video. What do you think they will be about? Write your ideas below.

**Build Background:
Sea Turtles**

CRITICAL VOCABULARY

obsessed

disoriented

blunt

recruiting

appointed

stranded

On Sea Turtle Patrol

by **Nancy Dawson**

illustrated by **Denise Ortakales**

1 "Last call, Callie!" Gram jangles her keys as she heads out to the carport.

2 "Coming!" I yell, tossing off the covers. Outside my window the sky is awash with a predawn glow.

3 The trouble with tracking sea turtles is you have to get up early every day. Today is my twenty-fifth day on patrol, which Gram says is probably a record for a twelve-year-old.

4 When Dad dropped me off at Gram's here in Florida two days after school got out, who knew I would morph from a Cincinnati city kid into a turtle-obsessed beach volunteer? If I'm not out on the beach, I'm watching turtle videos or reading turtle books.

5 I pull on cargo shorts and my blue T-shirt, the one with baby turtles scrambling up the front and over the shoulders. I grab a banana off the kitchen counter and rush outside.

> **obsessed** If you are obsessed with something, you think about it all the time.

6 By the time Gram and I get to the beach, the sky glows pale yellow, with the sun peeking up over the edge of the horizon. I breathe in the salty air and lick the tangy taste off my lips. I stuff my flip-flops into my pockets and dig my toes into the white sand.

7 We walk along the water's edge, looking for fresh turtle tracks, which scientists call "crawls." The beachfront is lined with high-rise condos and hotels, but at this early hour no one's out except two joggers running at the edge of the surf. A noisy pack of brown pelicans is fighting over the carcass of a dead fish tangled in seaweed. The only other sound is the *whoosh*, *whoosh* of the waves rolling in and out.

8 "Fresh crawl!" I call out, proud to see turtle tracks before Gram does. The crawl emerges straight out of the ocean, two long lines of depressions in the sand dug out by the turtle's flippers.

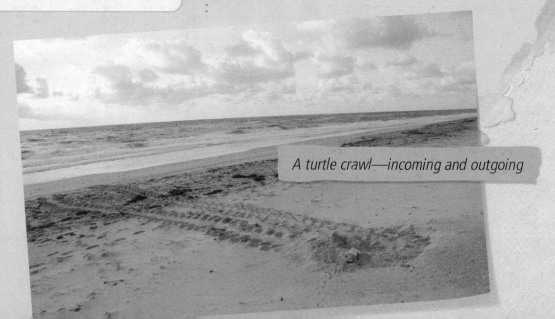

A turtle crawl—incoming and outgoing

9   "What kind of turtle? Which direction?" Gram demands.

10   I study the turtle crawl photos at the back of the clipboard before saying, "Loggerhead, incoming?" Loggerheads are the most common turtle on this stretch of Florida's Gulf Coast. I hold my breath and wait for Gram's verdict.

11   "Good call, Callie," she says. She records the nest location, date, and time on her clipboard. She frowns down at the sand. "Where's the outgoing crawl?"

12   I examine the sand. No outgoing crawl, which should be near the incoming tracks or even on top of them. Turtles can sometimes be disoriented by the bright lights of condos and hotels near the beach. Did this mama turtle lose her way?

> **disoriented**   Creatures that are disoriented are confused about where they are.

13   Gram stuffs her clipboard into her backpack. "Come on, Callie, let's follow her tracks."

14   The crawl leads us above the high tide line, where the sand is dry and loose. Seagrass tickles my bare legs as we follow the tracks up the face of a sand dune. We reach the top of the dune, where I see . . .

15   A turtle! She's lying in a slight depression in the sand, motionless. Her eyes are wide open, glassy-brown and rimmed with salt crystals.

16   "Is she OK?" I ask Gram.

17   "I hope so. She's probably resting between bouts of digging out her egg chamber," Gram says. "Keep watching."

241

18   I do, but the turtle just lies there. She's about three feet long and has the large head and big, blunt jaws of a loggerhead. Her shell, flippers, and head are covered in a maze of reddish-brown geometric shapes, each outlined by thin white lines. Patches of green algae and gray barnacles cling to her shell.

19   "Gram, look! She's moving her back flippers." The turtle pushes her hind flippers like alternating paddles, scooping out sand from beneath her rear end. She digs and rests, digs and rests.

> **blunt**   Something that is blunt is flat or rounded, rather than sharp.

20   To lay her eggs, she has to dig a nest chamber two feet deep. And she's taking forever! By now the sun is full up. I know the turtle is in a trance, unaware of us or anything happening around her until she is done nesting. But still, we have to keep her safe.

21   "Look! Eggs!" Gram says, pulling my attention back to the turtle. Her stubby tail moves to one side as she pushes out round, white eggs, each the size of a Ping-Pong ball. Clear, gloppy liquid slides off the eggs as they drop down into the nest chamber.

A nest with freshly laid eggs

22   "Wow!" I whisper. I feel like I'm starring in a TV nature show. Only the turtle is the real star.

23   "Sea turtles have been coming ashore to lay their eggs for millions of years, all over the earth," Gram says, her voice filled with awe.

24   The turtle is still pushing out eggs, one by one. She'll lay about 120 before she's done. Then she'll return to the sea.

25   *If* she makes it back across the beach. Nighttime is turtle time, but someone forgot to tell this turtle. What if she's confused by the daylight and can't find the ocean? What if she ends up in a hotel parking lot and gets squashed by a car?

26   My stomach knots up and my brain is stuck on terrible turtle troubles. What can we do?

27   Gram's on her phone, recruiting other volunteers to come to our location, quick. "We'll try to help her get back to her ocean home," she says to me. "After that, it's up to her."

> **recruiting**   If you are recruiting people, you are asking them to help do something.

28   The turtle's just lying there again. I wonder if she's sick or injured. But then she flips sand into the air and scoots her body around to pack it down over the nest hole. She scatters loose sand on top to hide her nest from marauding raccoons and stray dogs. Then she turns and crawls toward the sea, never looking back.

29   We're on the move, too.

30   "Callie, you patrol the left side, keeping ten feet away and behind her. I'll take the right side. We need to keep people away from her and off her incoming tracks, which she'll follow back to the sea."

31   My side of the beach is empty except for a flock of shorebirds down by the water's edge. They're pecking in the wet sand, hunting for insects and other tasty snacks. Each wave chases them to drier ground. As soon as the wave pulls out, they're back.

32   I turn away from the birds and watch the turtle. One flipper-step at a time, she slowly drags her 300-pound body forward. No wonder female loggerheads come on land only four or five times a summer to lay eggs. They spend the rest of their lives gracefully swimming around in the ocean.

33   Gram points to two men jogging at the edge of the waves. "Stay with the turtle while I go talk to those guys," she says.

34   After she goes I hear a yell down near the water. "Whooo-eee!" From the top of the dune, I spot two guys on bikes doing wheelies in the surf. They're headed straight for the turtle tracks.

35   I start running, but my feet can't get much traction on the loose sand. I'm moving, well, as slow as a turtle. When I get to the wet sand, the running is easier. "Stop!" I yell, flinging my arms out like a traffic cop.

36   "Who appointed you beach police?" a guy with black, spiky hair demands. He's a foot taller than I am, and older, probably in high school. His buddy closes in from the left.

37   I clear my throat and think back to my volunteer training: *Introduce yourself. Turn bystanders into allies.*

38   "I'm Callie. I'm not the beach police, but I am a trained turtle volunteer. We have a stranded sea turtle. Can you help?"

39   "Definitely!" the buddy says. "I'm Eric." He points to the spiky-haired guy. "That's Mateo. Last year in biology, we adopted a turtle nest. We got to go dig it up three days after the turtles busted out, and we took inventory by counting the number of hatched eggs."

40   I am so jealous, but all I say is, "Great!"

41   Eric scans the beach. "Turtle!" he whoops, pointing.

42   The turtle flops over the top of the sand dune and skids down its steep front. Then she waddles forward, pulling herself with her flippers.

43   A group of adults with three little kids in tow stream out of a condo. They're carrying fold-up chairs and an umbrella and dragging a cooler. I have to stop them before they trample the turtle tracks. I slap on my Save the Turtles visor, hoping it makes me look older and more official.

appointed   If you are appointed to a job, you are assigned to or chosen for it.

stranded   If you are stranded, you are stuck somewhere without a way to leave.

44 "I'm going to go talk to those people," I tell Eric and Mateo. "You guys please patrol along this side of the tracks. Anyone who comes along, ask them to stay ten feet back from the turtle and off her tracks."

45 I run over to the approaching people and tell them about the sea turtle. They're tourists from Iowa and really excited by the chance to see a turtle. They pile their equipment in a heap and follow me.

46 Eric and Mateo are standing guard beside the crawl, scanning the beach and watching the turtle's slow progress. I spread the Iowa people out in a line next to them.

47 Gram and the joggers are lined up along the other side of the tracks. Some sea turtle volunteers have arrived and are working both sides, all in their official lime green "Sea Turtle Volunteer" T-shirts. I so want one of those T-shirts, but I can't have one until I'm eighteen, old enough to be an official volunteer.

48 A crowd attracts a crowd, that's what Gram always says. Suddenly we have about twenty or thirty people on each side of the tracks. They hold out their phones and take pictures of the turtle, of themselves, of the volunteers, and of me.

49 A woman stands apart, her eyes focused on the turtle. With her arms, she beckons the turtle forward, as though to say: *Come on, you can do it!*

50 And she can. I think. Only fifteen feet to go before the turtle will meet the edge of the incoming waves. All the official turtle volunteers are down by the water now, so I go there, too.

51 With a final thrust, the turtle meets an incoming wave. Water pours over her body. But then the wave whooshes out, leaving the turtle stranded in the wet sand. I want to run to her and push her forward, but I know not to. The volunteers spread out their arms to keep people back, so I do, too.

52 Another wave washes over the turtle, and then another, and then she is floating free. She glides under the water and is gone.

53 Everyone cheers and claps. A little kid yells, "Bye-bye turtle!" Strangers hug and cry, and I find my own cheeks are wet.

54 Gram puts an arm around my shoulders. "Good job, Callie. I'm proud of you." We stand there, Gram and me, staring out at the infinite ocean.

55 My Best Turtle Patrol Day. Ever!

Saving the Kemp's Ridley Sea Turtle

As you watch *Saving the Kemp's Ridley Sea Turtle,* notice how the narration and the visuals work together to give information. How does the narrator introduce new information about sea turtles? How is this information supported by visuals? How is the information in the video similar to what you learned in *On Sea Turtle Patrol?* Take notes in the space below.

Why have the turtles become endangered? What steps have scientists taken to save the Kemp's Ridley sea turtle? How long did the scientists have to wait to see the results of their efforts? Write your responses in the space below.

Collaborative Discussion

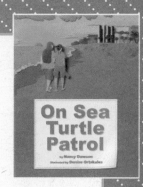

Look back at what you wrote on page 238. Tell a partner two things you learned from the text and video. Then work with a group to discuss the questions. Look for details and examples in *On Sea Turtle Patrol* and *Saving the Kemp's Ridley Sea Turtle*. Choose someone in your group to take notes on your discussion.

1 Reread page 245. Why does Callie ask Eric and Mateo for help?

2 Why do scientists and volunteers look for turtle tracks?

3 How are people helping increase the population of sea turtles?

Listening Tip

If you are the note-taker, listen carefully to each speaker. When the speaker finishes, jot down the central ideas that he or she shared.

Speaking Tip

After discussing each question, ask the note-taker to read back the group's responses. Decide together if anyone has something more to add.

Write a Response

Respond to the Text and Video *On Sea Turtle Patrol* and *Saving the Kemp's Ridley Sea Turtle* explain the steps people are taking to protect endangered sea turtles. What actions do these people take? How do they show that they care for their environment? Cite evidence from the text and video to support your response. Try to use some of the Big Idea Words in your writing.

List ideas from the text and the video that tell what people are doing to save sea turtles. Note how these people show that they care for their environment.

WRITE ....

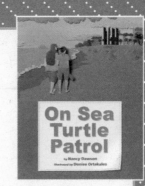

On Sea Turtle Patrol
by Nancy Dawson
Illustrated by Denise Ortakales

Now write your response in a paragraph.

✓ **Make sure your response**

☐	uses details from the text and video to answer the questions.
☐	explains what people are doing to protect sea turtles.
☐	shows how these people care for their environment.
☐	uses some of the Big Idea Words.
☐	is written in complete sentences.

Notice &
Note
Numbers and
Stats

Prepare to Read

GENRE STUDY **Informational texts** give facts and examples about a topic. In **argumentative texts,** an author states a claim about a topic and supports it with facts and details to convince readers to agree with the author's argument.

- Authors of informational texts may organize their ideas using headings and subheadings.

- Authors of informational texts may also organize ideas by stating a problem and explaining its solution.

- Argumentative texts include evidence, such as facts and examples, to support the author's argument.

SET A PURPOSE **Think about** the title and genre of the text. What do you know about how household trash affects our planet? What do you want to learn? Write your ideas below.

Build Background: Recycling

CRITICAL VOCABULARY

estimate

decay

252

How Can We Reduce Household Waste?

by Mary K. Pratt

HOUSEHOLD WASTE

1 Household waste includes all the trash created by the things we throw away. And we throw away many things. In the United States, the average person throws away about 4.5 pounds (2 kilograms) of stuff every day. Only 1.5 pounds (0.7 kg) of that gets recycled or composted. The remaining 3 pounds (1.4 kg) is household waste.

2 What happens when you add up all the household waste Americans create? It comes out to about 164 million tons (149 metric tons) each year. But this is only an **estimate** from the US government. No one knows the exact amount of household waste Americans create. In fact, some experts believe it might be up to seven times that amount! In any case, a huge number of unwanted items end up in the garbage. And all of this garbage has serious effects on our environment.

estimate If you give an estimate, you give an amount or size that is not exact.

AMERICAN WASTE
(including recyclables)

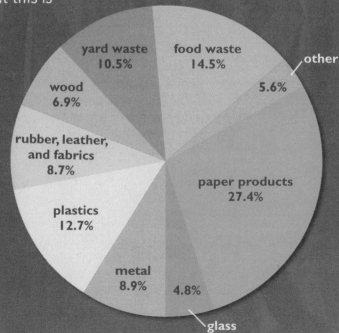

- yard waste 10.5%
- food waste 14.5%
- other 5.6%
- wood 6.9%
- paper products 27.4%
- rubber, leather, and fabrics 8.7%
- plastics 12.7%
- metal 8.9%
- glass 4.8%

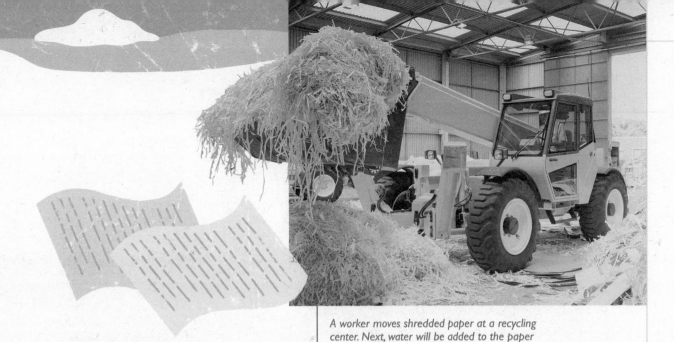

A worker moves shredded paper at a recycling center. Next, water will be added to the paper and it will be turned into pulp.

Types of Household Waste

3 There are four basic categories of household waste. The first category is paper, plastic, metal, and glass. The second category is food waste and yard waste. Cleaning products make up the third category. The fourth category is e-waste, or electronic waste. This includes items such as old cell phones and TVs.

4 Each of these types of waste has different effects on our planet. The good news is that we can fight the effects of every type of household waste. When we recycle and reuse waste, we keep these materials out of landfills. This helps clean the land, air, and water. It also improves our health. Let's explore each type of waste and find out what we can do to reduce its effects.

Plastic bottles decompose slowly in landfills. They should be recycled.

PAPER, PLASTIC, METAL, AND GLASS

5 Paper makes up more than one-quarter of the materials Americans throw away. Paper trash includes things such as notebooks and magazines. It also includes the cardboard and paper packages on the things we buy.

6 Another quarter of waste comes from plastic, metal, and glass. This includes items such as plastic bags and old toys. It also includes glass jars and metal cans. Soda cans are usually made of a metal called aluminum. Foods such as beans and soup usually come in cans made of steel.

Newspapers are one type of paper trash. What are some others?

Americans recycle 71 percent of their steel cans. But they recycle only 50 percent of their aluminum cans.

Effects of Pollution from Paper, Plastic, Metal, and Glass

7 When products are thrown away, they often end up in landfills. These are places where trash is buried in the ground. Other trash items are burned in incinerators.

8 Landfills and incinerators cause problems for our planet. For instance, when paper rots in landfills or burns in incinerators, it sends out greenhouse gases. These gases trap heat in Earth's atmosphere. Greenhouse gases are important because they make our planet warm enough for life. But too much greenhouse gas leads to higher temperatures.

9 Things made of plastic take a long time to decompose, or break down into smaller bits. So these products stay as they are for hundreds of years and take up space in landfills. They often leach, or leak, dangerous chemicals into the environment. When plastic is burned in incinerators, it releases chemicals into the air. Many of these chemicals are harmful to people and plants.

In the United States, more than half of all waste ends up in landfills.

257

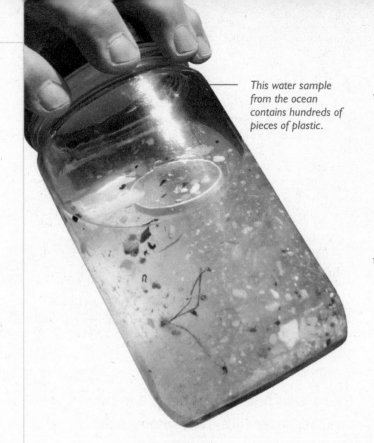

This water sample from the ocean contains hundreds of pieces of plastic.

10   Sometimes trash does not even make it into landfills or incinerators. Many household items end up as litter in parks, forests, rivers, lakes, and oceans. The litter problem is so big that vast sections of the ocean are covered with bits of plastic.

11   All that litter puts toxic chemicals into the land, water, and air. This can make plants and animals, including humans, very sick. Animals can also get trapped in plastic trash and starve. Sometimes animals eat small pieces of trash because they think it is food. These animals often get sick and die as a result.

What Can We Do?

12 You can reduce the amount of trash you create. Start by buying only what you need. When you do buy something, look for items made from recycled materials. Also, look for products that have little or no packaging. One good choice is buying whole fruits and vegetables instead of those in boxes or bags. When shopping, bring reusable bags instead of using disposable plastic bags.

13 When you are ready to get rid of something, look for ways to reuse it. For example, an old shoe box can become a storage bin. If you do not want an item that is in good condition, give it to someone else. If no one wants it, try to recycle it. If you have to throw it out, dispose of it properly so it does not become litter.

One way to reuse an old can is to make it into a flowerpot.

Different types of plastic are given different numbers. Numbers 2, 4, and 5 are the least harmful to people and to the environment.

14   People are also finding ways to make better use of all our trash. For example, some clothing is made from recycled plastic bottles. Scientists are also studying whether a certain fungus can eat a common type of plastic. That would help cut back on all the plastic trash that fills up landfills.

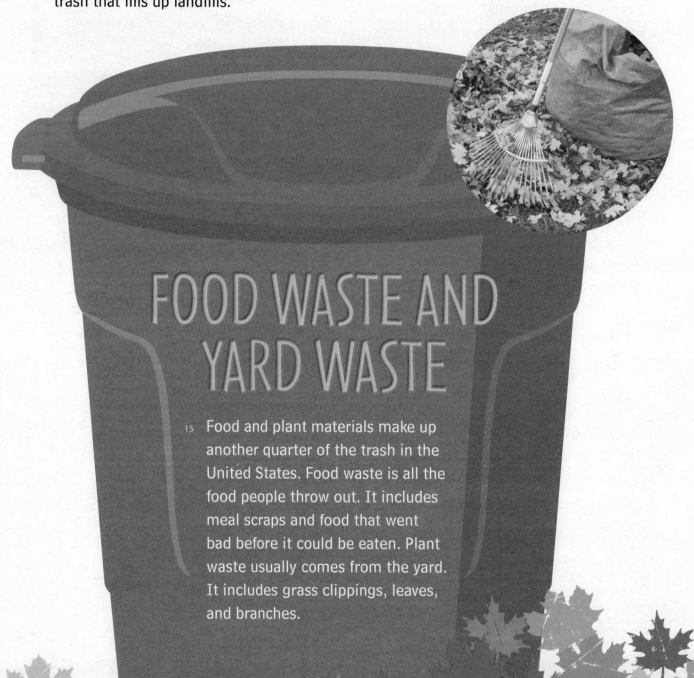

FOOD WASTE AND YARD WASTE

15   Food and plant materials make up another quarter of the trash in the United States. Food waste is all the food people throw out. It includes meal scraps and food that went bad before it could be eaten. Plant waste usually comes from the yard. It includes grass clippings, leaves, and branches.

Effects of Food Waste and Yard Waste Pollution

16 In the United States, farmers produce more than 590 billion pounds (268 billion kg) of food every year. But Americans waste between one-quarter and one-half of that food. Farmers sometimes let fruits and vegetables rot in fields. They often do this when the food is not an ideal shape or color, because this makes it harder to sell.

17 Stores throw away a lot of food, too. They want customers to have plenty of choices. So, they stock more food than they plan to sell. They also get rid of many foods that do not look perfect.

18 People waste a lot of food at home as well. Families often fail to use their food before it goes bad. And many people buy more food than they can use. When food and yard waste ends up in landfills, it rots. This creates methane, a powerful greenhouse gas.

These tomatoes have skin cracks, so the farmer left them in the field.

A woman in Seattle shows her three waste bins.
Waste in the two large bins will be recycled.
Waste in the small black bin will end up in a landfill.

Solutions to Food Waste and Yard Waste Pollution

19 How can you help? Take only the food that you plan to eat. And try not to be too picky. For instance, cut a bruise out of an apple and eat the rest instead of throwing away the whole apple.

20   Governments are getting involved, too. The city of Seattle, Washington passed a law in 2015. It requires people to recycle food waste. The city fines people who do not follow the law.

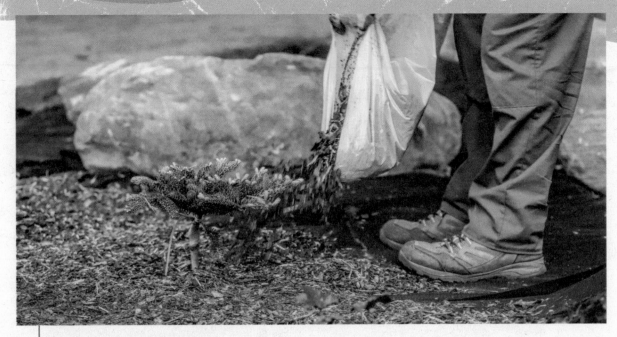

Mulch can be made from many things, including wood chips, grass clippings, and hay.

21   People can generate less yard waste by keeping leaves and grass clippings on the lawn. These materials provide natural nutrition to the landscape. People can shred leaves and grass clippings to make mulch. Mulch is a layer of material that is spread over the ground. It keeps the soil healthier.

22   You can also turn food and yard waste into dirt. This process is called composting. Some people use special bins for their food scraps and yard waste. Other people simply make a pile out in the open. Over time, these materials will naturally decay and turn into dirt. Then you can use the dirt to plant a garden!

decay   When things decay, they slowly break down and rot.

Composting usually takes two to six months.

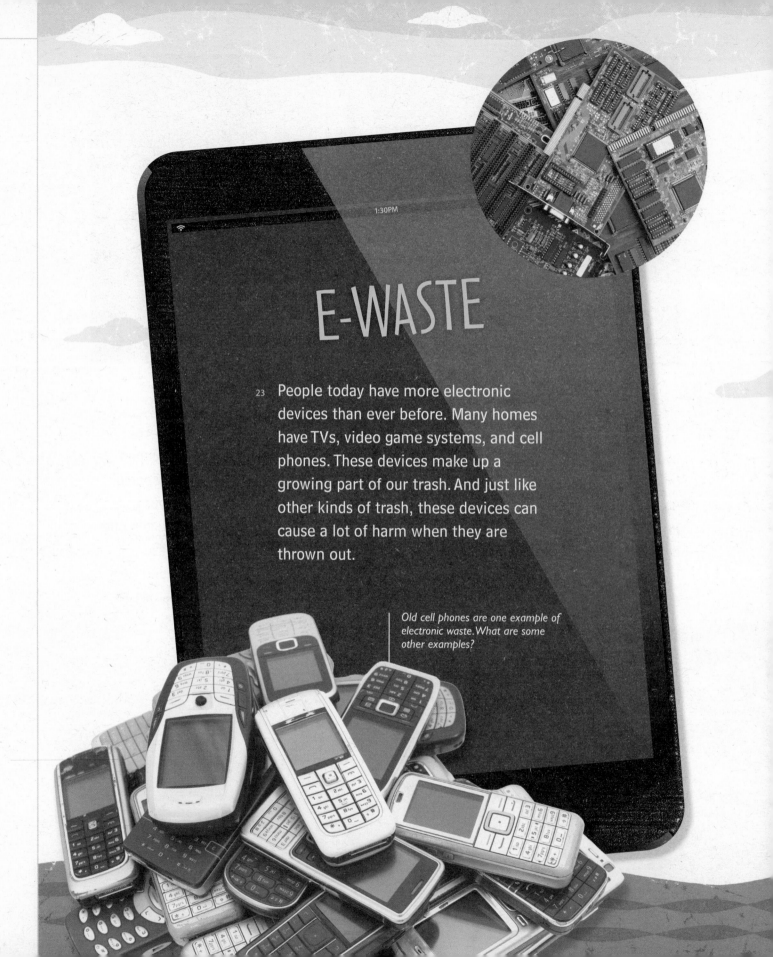

E-WASTE

23 People today have more electronic devices than ever before. Many homes have TVs, video game systems, and cell phones. These devices make up a growing part of our trash. And just like other kinds of trash, these devices can cause a lot of harm when they are thrown out.

Old cell phones are one example of electronic waste. What are some other examples?

Take good care of your cell phone so it will last a long time.

Effects of E-Waste Pollution

24 Electronic waste, or e-waste, contains many toxic materials. But less than 15 percent of e-waste is recycled. That means most e-waste ends up in landfills or incinerators. When e-waste is buried or burned, the toxic materials can be released into the land, water, and air.

25 E-waste contains a high amount of lead. If e-waste is not disposed of properly, lead can leach into people's water supplies. When people drink this water, it can damage their kidneys. It also damages their blood and their nervous systems.

Solutions to E-Waste Pollution

26 You can reduce harmful e-waste. First, do not get rid of electronics that still work. Second, when you do get rid of electronics, look for recycling programs at local stores and government offices. These programs should guarantee that the e-waste will be handled responsibly. If your favorite electronics company does not have a recycling program, ask the company to start one.

REDUCE, REUSE, RECYCLE

27 You can help stop household waste pollution by following the three Rs: reduce, reuse, and recycle. These Rs are listed in order of importance. That means the most important step is reduce. The less we buy, the less trash we produce.

A worker operates a machine at a recycling center.

28 So the next time you are at the store, think about what you really need. If you can live without something, consider leaving it on the shelf.

29 The second most important step is reuse. When you do buy something, try to use it until it wears out. And if you do not need it anymore, give it to someone who will use it. That way, it will not go to a landfill.

30 The third most important step is recycle. When it is time to get rid of something, make every effort to recycle it rather than throwing it in the trash. In most areas, waste disposal companies provide separate recycling bins. So people can easily recycle paper, glass, and some kinds of plastic and metal. Some items, such as paint and batteries, are harder to recycle. But many areas have centers where these items can be brought for recycling.

Do you have old toys that you do not use? Consider giving them to younger kids instead of throwing them away.

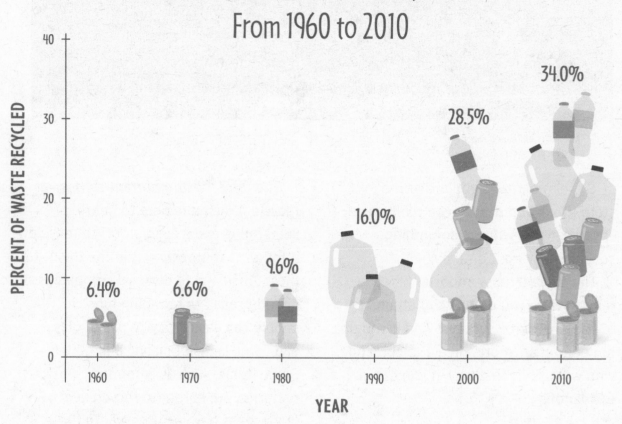

American Recycling Rates
From 1960 to 2010

PERCENT OF WASTE RECYCLED

6.4% 6.6% 9.6% 16.0% 28.5% 34.0%

1960 1970 1980 1990 2000 2010

YEAR

Working Together to Find Solutions

31　Many places have laws that require people to recycle. The city of Austin, Texas has set a goal to cut the amount of trash it sends to landfills to nearly zero by the year 2040. The country of Sweden has nearly achieved this goal. It sends only 1 percent of its trash to landfills.

32　　Household waste is a major problem. But we have the power to solve it. And the solution begins with making smart choices in our everyday lives.

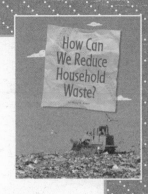

Collaborative Discussion

Look back at what you wrote on page 252. Tell a partner two things you learned from this text. Then work with a group to discuss the questions below. Refer to details and examples in *How Can We Reduce Household Waste?* to explain your answers. Take notes for your responses. When you speak, use your notes.

1 Review pages 257–258. What are some of the ways that trash harms people, plants, and animals?

2 Reread page 261. What are some reasons that food is wasted in the United States each year?

3 How can people reduce the amount of trash they create?

Listening Tip

Show others that you are listening and care about what they say. Look at the speaker and smile or nod when you agree with an idea.

Speaking Tip

If someone says something interesting or helpful, tell that person that you like his or her idea. You can also say why you like it.

269

Write a Response

Respond to the Text In *How Can We Reduce Household Waste?*, you learned how people's trash affects our planet. Think about the things people can do to reduce household waste. What actions can they take? How can these actions help the planet? Cite evidence from the text to support your response.

EVIDENCE

List ideas from *How Can We Reduce Household Waste?* that tell what people can do to help reduce household waste.

WRITE

Now write your response in a paragraph.

✓ **Make sure your response**

☐ answers the questions.

☐ uses evidence from the text.

☐ describes what people can do to reduce household waste.

☐ explains how reducing waste helps care for the planet.

☐ is written in complete sentences.

Notice & Note
Tough Questions

Prepare to Read

GENRE STUDY   A **biography** is the story of a real person's life written by someone other than that person.

- Authors of biographies present events in chronological order.

- Authors of biographies may use literary language and devices to present major events in a person's life.

- Biographies include third-person pronouns such as *he, she, him, her, his, hers, they, them,* and *their*.

SET A PURPOSE   **Think about** the title and genre of this text. What do you think the subject of the biography is known for? What are some things you would like to learn about this person? Write your ideas below.

CRITICAL VOCABULARY

ancestors

swirled

currents

sneered

outspoken

canopy

envision

Meet the Author:
Jen Cullerton Johnson
Meet the Illustrator:
Sonia Lynn Sadler

SEEDS OF CHANGE

by
Jen Cullerton Johnson

illustrated by
Sonia Lynn Sadler

1. "Come," Wangari's mother called. She beckoned her young daughter over to a tall tree with a wide, smooth trunk and a crown of green, oval leaves.

2. "Feel," her mother whispered.

3. Wangari spread her small hands over the tree's trunk. She smoothed her fingers over the rough bark.

4. "This is the *mugumo*," her mother said. "It is home to many. It feeds many, too."

5. She snapped off a wild fig from a low branch and gave it to her daughter. Wangari ate the delicious fruit, just as geckos and elephants did. High in the tree, birds chirped in their nests. The branches bounced with jumping monkeys.

6. "Our people, the Kikuyu of Kenya, believe that our ancestors rest in the tree's shade," her mother explained.

7. Wangari wrapped her arms around the trunk as if hugging her great-grandmother's spirit. She promised never to cut down the tree.

ancestors Your ancestors are the people in your family who lived long ago.

8   Each year the mugumo grew, and so did Wangari. As the oldest girl in her family, she had many chores. Every day she fetched water, clear and sweet, from the river. In the rainy season she planted sweet potatoes, millet, and beans. When the sun shone brightly in the dry season, she shooed the chickens into the shade.

9   Sometimes when her brother, Nderitu, returned from school, he and Wangari played among the arrowroot plants by the stream, where thousands of eggs hatched into tadpoles and tadpoles turned into frogs. During those times, Nderitu told Wangari what he had learned in his classes. "Plants give air for people to breathe," he said. "Twenty divided by two is ten. There are seven great seas to sail."

10 Wangari listened as still as a tree, but her mind swirled with curiosity like the currents in the stream. Even though she knew few Kikuyu girls who could read, Wangari dreamed of going to school and learning, just like her brother.

11 "I must go to school," she told him.

12 "You will," he promised.

13 Nderitu talked to their parents. "Why doesn't Wangari go to school?" he asked.

swirled   If something swirled, it moved quickly around in circles.
currents Currents are flowing movements of water in a lake, river, or ocean.

14   Wangari's parents knew she was smart and a hard worker. Although it was unusual for a girl to be educated, they decided to send her to school. They knew she would not disappoint them. After some time to arrange for fees and supplies, Wangari's mother came to her. "You are going to school," she told her daughter.

15   Wangari grinned widely and hugged her mother. "Thank you!" she cried. "I will make you proud."

16   Wangari walked the long road to a one-room schoolhouse with walls made of mud, a floor of dirt, and a roof of tin. In time she learned to copy her letters and trace numbers. Wangari's letters soon made words, and her words made sentences. She learned how numbers could be added and subtracted, multiplied and divided. Animals and plants, she discovered, were like human beings in many ways. They needed air, water, and nourishment too.

17   When Wangari finished elementary school, she was eleven years old. Her mind was like a seed rooted in rich soil, ready to grow. Wangari wanted to continue her education, but to do so she would have to leave her village and move to the capital city of Nairobi. Wangari had never been farther than her valley's ridge. She was scared.

18 "Go," her mother said. She picked up a handful of earth and placed it gently into her daughter's hand. "Where you go, we go."

19 Wangari was sad to leave, but she knew that what her mother said was true. Wherever Wangari went, so went her family, her village, and her Kikuyu ways. She kissed her family and said good-bye to the mugumo tree, remembering her promise always to protect it.

20 Wangari's new life in the city amazed her. Skyscrapers towered above her head, not trees. People rushed through the streets like river water over stones. At school she lived with other girls like her, all trying to weave their village customs with new city ones. At night when the girls slept, Wangari dreamed of home and the sweet figs of the mugumo tree. Her dreams reminded her to honor her Kikuyu tradition of respecting all living things.

21   Wangari was an excellent student, and science became her favorite subject. She especially loved studying living things. Air, she learned, was made from two molecules of oxygen bonded together. Bodies were made up of cells. Leaves changed color because of photosynthesis.

22   As graduation neared, Wangari told her friends she wanted to become a biologist.

23   "Not many native women become scientists," they told her.

24   "I will," she said.

25   Wangari would have to travel halfway around the world to the United States to study biology. She had never left Kenya and had little money. But with her teachers' help, she won a scholarship to a college in Kansas.

26   America was very different from Kenya. In college, many of Wangari's science professors were women. From them she learned that a woman could do anything she wanted to, even if it hadn't been done before. While Wangari discovered how molecules move under a microscope lens and how cells divide in petri dishes, she also found her strength as a woman scientist.

27   After she graduated from college, Wangari traveled to Pennsylvania to continue her studies. Letters from home told Wangari about changes in Kenya. The people had elected a Kikuyu president, Jomo Kenyatta. Proud of her country and proud to be Kikuyu, Wangari decided to return home to Kenya to help her people.

28   America had changed Wangari. She had discovered a spirit of possibility and freedom that she wanted to share with Kenyan women. She accepted a teaching job at the University of Nairobi. Not many women were professors then, and even fewer taught science. Wangari led the way for other women and girls. She worked for equal rights so that female scientists would be treated with the same respect as male scientists.

myNotes

29   Wangari watched sadly as her government sold more and more land to big foreign companies that cut down forests for timber and to clear land for coffee plantations. Native trees, such as cedar and acacia, vanished. Without trees, birds had no place to nest. Monkeys lost their swings. Tired mothers walked miles for firewood.

30   When Wangari visited her village she saw that the Kikuyu custom of not chopping down the mugumo trees had been lost. No longer held in place by tree roots, the soil streamed into the rivers. The water that had been used to grow maize, bananas, and sweet potatoes turned to mud and dried up. Many families went hungry.

31   Wangari could not bear to think of the land being destroyed. Now married and the mother of three children, she worried about what would happen to all the mothers and children who depended on the land.

32   "We must do something," Wangari said.

33   Wangari had an idea as small as a seed but as tall as a tree that reaches for the sky. "*Harabee!* Let's work together!" she said to her countrywomen—mothers like her. Wangari dug deep into the soil, a seedling by her side. "We must plant trees."

34   Many women listened. Many planted seedlings. Some men laughed and sneered. Planting trees was women's work, they said. Others complained that Wangari was too outspoken—with too many opinions and too much education for a woman.

35   Wangari refused to listen to those who criticized her.

sneered   If you sneered, you showed disapproval and lack of respect by the look on your face.
outspoken   If you are outspoken, you say what you think even when others do not agree.

36   Instead she told them, "Those trees you are cutting down today were not planted by you but by those who came before. You must plant trees that will benefit the community to come, like a seedling with sun, good soil, and abundant rain, the roots of our future will bury themselves in the ground and a canopy of hope will reach the sky."

37   Wangari traveled to villages, towns, and cities with saplings and seeds, shovels and hoes. At each place she went, women planted rows of trees that looked like green belts across the land. Because of this they started calling themselves the Green Belt Movement.

38   "We might not change the big world but we can change the landscape of the forest," she said.

39   One tree turned to ten, ten to one hundred, one hundred to one million, all the way up to thirty million planted trees. Kenya grew green again. Birds nested in new trees. Monkeys swung on branches. Rivers filled with clean water. Wild figs grew heavy in mugumo branches.

> **canopy**   A canopy is a rooflike covering, like the top branches of trees in a forest.

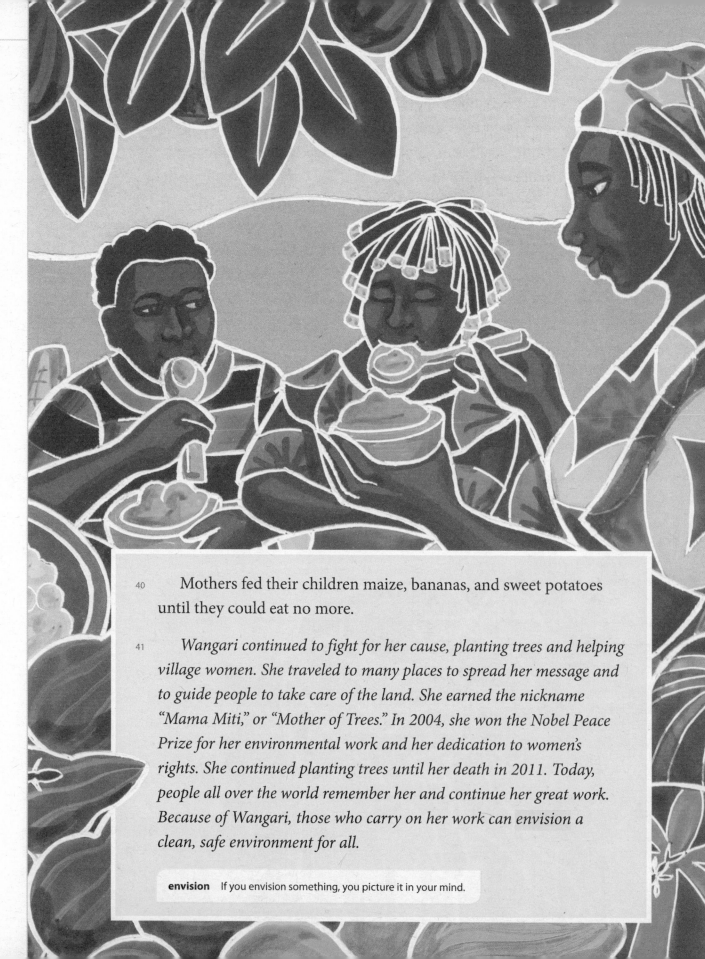

40   Mothers fed their children maize, bananas, and sweet potatoes until they could eat no more.

41   *Wangari continued to fight for her cause, planting trees and helping village women. She traveled to many places to spread her message and to guide people to take care of the land. She earned the nickname "Mama Miti," or "Mother of Trees." In 2004, she won the Nobel Peace Prize for her environmental work and her dedication to women's rights. She continued planting trees until her death in 2011. Today, people all over the world remember her and continue her great work. Because of Wangari, those who carry on her work can envision a clean, safe environment for all.*

envision   If you envision something, you picture it in your mind.

Collaborative Discussion

Look back at what you wrote on page 272. Tell a partner two things you learned from this text. Then work with a group to discuss the questions below. Support your answers with details and examples from *Seeds of Change*. Take notes for your responses. When you speak, use your notes.

1. Reread page 277. How is Wangari's life different from her brother's? How does her brother help her?

2. Review page 282. What new ideas does Wangari learn in the United States?

Listening Tip

Wait for your turn to speak. As you listen, write down any questions you want to ask once the speaker has finished talking.

3. What problems does Wangari hope to solve by planting trees?

Speaking Tip

Always make suggestions in a helpful way. Say things like "Another way to think about it is …" or "I can see why you think that, but …"

Cite Text Evidence

Write a Response

PROMPT . . . .

Respond to the Text In *Seeds of Change,* you read about the life of environmentalist and Nobel Peace Prize winner Wangari Maathai. Think about the work that Wangari Maathai did. What actions did she take to protect her environment? How did her actions help care for the planet? Cite evidence from the text to support your response.

EVIDENCE . . . .

List ideas from *Seeds of Change* that tell what Wangari Maathai did to protect her environment and care for the planet.

Now write your response in a paragraph.

✓ **Make sure your response**

☐	answers the questions.
☐	uses evidence from the text.
☐	describes what Wangari Maathai did to protect her environment.
☐	explains how Wangari's actions helped care for the planet.
☐	is written in complete sentences.

? Essential Question

What can people do to care for our planet?

Write an Opinion Essay

PROMPT Think about what you learned from the selections in this module. Why is it important to care for our planet? What environmentally friendly actions can individuals take? Use evidence from the selections to write an opinion essay about why people should care for the planet. Use some of the Big Idea Words from this module in your writing.

✓ Make sure your opinion essay
☐ states your opinion in the introduction.
☐ explains what people can do to care for the planet.
☐ uses text evidence and examples from the selections.
☐ includes transitions to link ideas.
☐ provides a conclusion.

Think about what you learned in this module about caring for the planet. What are some actions people can take to help the environment? Use evidence from the module selections to support your opinion. Use the chart below to plan your writing.

Actions	Supporting Evidence

DRAFT .... Write your opinion essay.

Use the information you wrote on page 293 to draft your opinion essay. Write an **introduction** that states your opinion.

[ ]

Write a **body paragraph** that includes reasons for your opinion. Cite evidence from the module selections that supports each reason. Use transitions to connect your ideas.

[ ]

Write a **conclusion** that restates your opinion and summarizes your ideas.

[ ]

The revision and editing steps give you a chance to look carefully at your draft and make changes. Work with a partner to determine whether you have clearly supported your opinion and explained your ideas. Use these questions to help you.

✓ PURPOSE/FOCUS	ORGANIZATION	EVIDENCE/SUPPORT	ELABORATION	CONVENTIONS
☐ Have I clearly stated my opinion? ☐ Did I explain why it is important to care for our planet?	☐ Does my opinion have a clear introduction? ☐ Does my conclusion summarize the reasons for my opinion?	☐ Did I include text evidence and examples from the selections to support my opinion?	☐ Did I use transition words to connect ideas? ☐ Did I use some of the Big Idea Words in my writing?	☐ Have I used correct punctuation and capitalization? ☐ Did I indent each new paragraph? ☐ Have I spelled all the words correctly?

PUBLISH ····························· Create a finished copy.

Create a Finished Copy Make a final copy of your opinion essay. Write legibly using your cursive writing skills.

Communication Nation

"Write to be understood, speak
to be heard, read to grow."

—Lawrence Clark Powell

What forms can communication take?

Get Curious

Video

Languages

Communication

Advances
in Technology
Throughout History

How Technology Has Changed Communication

myNotes

Timeline of Communications Technology

This timeline shows when important communication devices became popular in the United States.

The **telegraph** sent messages long distances over wires. Telegraph operators tapped out messages in Morse code, a system of dots and dashes that stand for letters.

1850s

The **telephone** has been called the greatest invention of the 19th century. People no longer had to be in the same room to talk to one another!

1870s

After **television** was invented, people could see events as they happened. Television brought people together to witness important moments in history.

1950s

1860s

Before the **typewriter**, people wrote letters and other documents by hand. The typewriter made writing a book or other lengthy publication much faster.

1920s

In the 1920s, everyone wanted a **radio** for their living room. Families gathered around it to hear a news or entertainment broadcast.

1 Imagine it's 1866, and your family has just arrived in Houston, Texas, after a long trip by ship. Your grandmother in New York City is anxious to hear from you. So you pull out paper, a pen, and ink. You dip the pen nib in ink and write a letter by hand. You take it to the post office. It will travel on a ship that's leaving for New York City at the end of the week, and about 2,300 miles and weeks later, your letter will reach your grandmother!

2 Fast forward to the present. Your family has just arrived in Houston. You borrow your mom's cell phone and text, "We made it!" to your grandmother in New York City, along with a photo of the Houston skyline. She gets your message almost instantly and texts back, "Have fun! See you next week!"

Personal computers changed the way people work by allowing users to store and share information over computer networks.

1970s

When the **World Wide Web** came along, it was like a giant electronic information library. Later it grew to include online stores, cat videos, and just about anything else imaginable

1990s

People use **social media** to connect and communicate. Through blogs, websites, and apps, people share photos and information about their lives.

2010s

1980s

The first **mobile phones** allowed people to talk on the go. Starting in the 1990s, mobile phones, now known as cell (or cellular) phones, let people text, too.

Email, short for *electronic mail*, is a tool for sending documents and photos from computer to computer. It's a fast, easy way to correspond with people anywhere in the world.

2000s

Smartphones are mini computers that allow users to email, search for information, buy things, listen to music, take photos and videos—and, yes, make phone calls.

Notice &
Note
3 Big Questions

Prepare to Read

GENRE STUDY **Informational texts** give facts and examples about a topic.

- Authors of informational texts may present their ideas in chronological order.

- Informational texts include visuals, such as charts, diagrams, graphs, timelines, and maps.

- Social studies texts also include words that are specific to the topic. These are words that name things or ideas.

SET A PURPOSE **Think about** the title and genre of this text. What do you know about the history of communication? What are some things you'd like to learn? Write your ideas below.

CRITICAL VOCABULARY

significantly

enabled

patent

peak

transmitted

plucked

proposed

influence

Build Background: Communication Today

The *History of* Communication

illustrations by Danny Schlitz

What Is Communication?

1   Communication is the sharing of ideas and information. People can share information through spoken and written words, by making and looking at images, and by making and listening to sounds. People can also communicate through gestures and facial expressions.

2   Over time, people have developed ways to share information with many people at once. Such methods of mass communication have included books, magazines, newspapers, television, radio, and, more recently, the Internet. Communication also takes place through sound recordings, motion pictures, and signs. Taken together, these tools allow people all over the world to communicate with one another.

The Printing Press

3   Between 1300 and 1600, a cultural movement called the Renaissance (rebirth) swept across Europe. The Renaissance was a period of great advancement in educational and artistic ideas, and it created a huge demand for books. Hand copying and block printing could not keep up with this demand.

4   In about 1440, a German inventor named Johannes (yoh-HAHN-uhs) Gutenberg developed a printing press that used movable type. Gutenberg made separate pieces of metal type for each letter of the alphabet. He assembled the pieces in a frame to form pages and applied ink to the type. The machine pressed the inked type against paper to print words.

This English engraving shows a steam-driven printing press from 1826.

Johannes Gutenberg

Newspapers are printed by the thousands, like these copies of the Houston Chronicle.

5   The Gutenberg press could print about 300 copies of a page daily. By 1500, there were more than 1,000 print shops in Europe, and several million books had been produced.

6   Printing quickly became an important communication tool. It significantly increased the production of religious texts. In addition, debates about social problems, religious beliefs, and government matters quickly appeared in print.

7   There were few changes to the printing press from Gutenberg's time until the 1800s. In 1811, a German named Friedrich König invented a steam-powered press that could print about 1,100 sheets per hour. In 1846, Richard Hoe of the United States invented a press that used rotating cylinders (revolving drums) to print 8,000 sheets per hour. Later models turned out as many as 20,000 sheets per hour.

8   The printing press is one of the most important inventions in history. It has enabled millions of people to receive knowledge through books, newspapers, magazines, and other printed formats.

significantly   If something changes significantly, the change is great enough to be noticed or important.

enabled   If you are enabled to do something, you are given a chance to do it.

The **Telegraph**

9   By the mid-1800s, people could share ideas through books, newspapers, and other written texts. However, there was still no way for people to communicate quickly if they were located in two different places. This would begin to change with the arrival of the electric telegraph, which could send messages by using electric current traveling along wires.

10   In 1820, a Danish scientist named Hans Christian Oersted (UR-stehd) found that an electric current can cause a magnetized needle to move. This discovery led to the invention of the telegraph. In communication by telegraph, an operator would send a message by using a special device to vary the electric current flowing through the wires. When the amount of electricity changed, a device at the receiving end would convert the signals into a specific series of clicks. An operator would then decode these clicks into words, or a telegram.

11   A number of inventors created early telegraphic devices, but the American painter and inventor Samuel F. B. Morse is credited with making the first practical telegraph in 1837. Morse received a U.S. patent for it in 1840.

> **patent**   If you have a patent for an invention, you are the only one who is allowed to make or sell the invention.

However, Morse's invention built upon years of research and experiments by people who came before him.

12   The telegraph became an important way to send information quickly to different locations. Reporters used the telegraph to send stories to their newspapers. Armies on both sides of the American Civil War (1861–1865) also relied heavily on the invention. The number of telegrams sent in the United States reached its peak in 1929, when more than 200 million were transmitted.

> **peak**   A peak is the highest point of something.
>
> **transmitted**   If something is transmitted, it is sent electronically from one place to another.

Samuel F. B. Morse

13   Samuel F. B. Morse was born on April 27, 1791, in Massachusetts. He received the patent for the first successful electric telegraph in the United States in 1840. He also invented Morse code, a system of sending messages using short and long sounds combined in various ways.

The **Telephone**

14 For most of the 1800s, there was no way for people at two distant locations to speak to each other directly. They could communicate only by sending letters or telegrams. But in the 1870s, a Scottish-born inventor named Alexander Graham Bell discovered a way to send people's voices across long distances.

15 In 1871, Bell arrived in Boston, Massachusetts, to become a teacher to people who were deaf. He performed experiments at night, working to improve the telegraph by creating a device that could send several telegraph messages over one wire at the same time.

16 On June 2, 1875, while conducting an experiment, Bell had a breakthrough. One of the metal reeds (thin pieces) on his device got stuck. Bell's assistant, Thomas Watson, plucked the reed to loosen it. In the other room, Bell heard the sound in his receiver.

> **plucked**   If something is plucked, it is pulled away from where it is.

Bell's telephone is shown here in illustrations from an English newspaper in 1877.

He realized that the vibrating reed had created changes to the electric current that passed through the wire. These changes were then reproduced in the receiver at the other end of the wire.

17   This discovery led to more experiments, and Bell received a patent for the first telephone on March 7, 1876. Three days later, he transmitted human speech over a telephone for the first time. In 1877, the Bell Telephone Company was founded. Within 10 years, there were more than 150,000 people who owned telephones in the United States.

18   Today, most people take the telephone for granted. With a worldwide network of telephone wires, it is easy for people to call someone in a different part of the world.

Alexander Graham Bell

19   Alexander Graham Bell (1847–1922) was born in Edinburgh, Scotland. His mother was a painter, and his father helped teach people who were deaf to speak. Bell also was an educator of deaf students, but he is best known as the inventor of the telephone.

20   Bell and his assistant, Thomas Watson, helped start telephone service in the United States. In 1877, Bell married Mabel Hubbard, one of his students, and they took the invention to England. But Bell did not stay in the telephone business. Instead, he preferred to continue his work with the deaf and to develop other inventions. Bell became a U.S. citizen in 1882.

Radio

21 The telegraph and the telephone enabled people at distant locations to communicate with each other, but only if the locations were connected by wires. This began to change in the late 1800s, when scientists discovered ways to send radio signals through the air. The invention of the radio allowed people to communicate quickly between any two points on land, at sea, and, later, in the sky and in space.

Guglielmo Marconi poses with his wireless radio receiver in 1896.

22 The development of the radio began in the 1830s with an idea proposed separately by an American professor named Joseph Henry and a British scientist named Michael Faraday. Both Henry and Faraday proposed that an electric current in one wire could produce an electric current in another wire, even when the wires are not connected.

23 Though many people contributed to the radio's development, Nikola Tesla, an American inventor from Austria Hungary, is credited with its invention. In 1891, he invented the Tesla coil, an extremely important component (part) of radio transmitters.

24 In 1895, an Italian inventor named Guglielmo Marconi (goo-LYEHL-moh mahr-KOH-nee) sent radio signals more than a mile through the air in the form of telegraph code signals. In 1901, Marconi's equipment transmitted signals all the way across the Atlantic Ocean, from England to Canada. In 1906, a Canadian-born scientist named Reginald Fessenden first transmitted voice by radio.

proposed   If you proposed an idea, you suggested that it was useful or true.

Families used to gather around the radio to listen to news, sports, and entertainment.

25   Radio broadcasting (programming) began on a large scale during the 1920s. Soon, families could gather in their living rooms to listen to comedies, adventure dramas, live music, variety shows, and other kinds of radio programming.

Nikola Tesla

26   Nikola Tesla (1856–1943) was born in Austria Hungary, in an area that is now part of Croatia. In 1884, Tesla left Europe for the United States. He worked for the inventor Thomas Edison but quit after one year.

27   Tesla became a pioneer in electrical technology, and he received more than 100 patents for a variety of inventions. His Tesla coil is still used in radio and television transmission today. Tesla's other achievements include groundbreaking work with X rays, radar, aircraft design, and neon and fluorescent lighting.

Television

28 By the early 1900s, when operators were first transmitting words by radio, many scientists had begun experimenting with the transmission of pictures. These experiments eventually led to the development of the television—a tremendously popular communication system that is used daily in nearly every corner of the world.

29 Many scientists contributed to the invention of television. Among them was Philo Farnsworth, an American scientist who created an electronic scanning system in 1922. This became a breakthrough in television technology.

Ways Television Signals Reach Homes

1 Satellites beam television signals to satellite dishes mounted outside homes.

2 Antennas on roofs or TV sets receive signals from local television stations.

3 Cable television signals are sent to homes through an underground cable.

30   Television works by changing pictures and sounds into electronic signals, which are then sent through the air. A television set receives these signals and turns them back into pictures and sounds.

31   As more families came to own television sets, TV programming began to influence people's attitudes and beliefs. By watching TV shows, viewers can see the latest fashions and hear the opinions of people with different backgrounds and beliefs. Through advertisements, people are encouraged to buy certain products. Television also plays a major role in how people learn about their government and select their leaders.

influence   If you influence people, you use your power or ability to change what they think.

Microwave signal

Communications satellite

Microwave signal

Microwave tower

Microwave tower

Communications satellites act as message relays as they orbit Earth.

The **Satellite**

32 A communications satellite is a type of satellite that receives radio, television, and other signals in space and relays (sends) them back to Earth.

33 Interestingly, a British science-fiction writer named Arthur C. Clarke is credited with inventing communications satellites. In an article published in 1945, Clarke described a satellite in orbit that could serve as an information relay station in the sky. This idea would turn out to be one of the greatest advances in modern communication.

34 Because a satellite is high above Earth, it can direct radio waves to any location within a large region. Without satellites, most radio transmissions could not reach far beyond the horizon (the distant, curved line where the land and sky appear to meet). Satellites can send messages to many places at once, and they offer instant service when radio links are needed quickly.

35 Early communications satellites were built to carry long-distance telephone calls. Satellites still perform this task today, providing

service in places where it is difficult to install telephone cables. Satellites also send telephone signals across oceans and to people in remote places. A ship's crew at sea, for instance, can talk to people anywhere in the world on mobile satellite phones.

36   Today, communications satellites also play a major role in television broadcasting. Satellites deliver programs to local cable TV companies or directly to homes. Satellite TV subscribers use dish-shaped antennas to receive hundreds of TV channels.

These large satellite dishes send and receive signals to and from space.

The **Internet**

37 Computers first came into practical use in the mid-1900s. However, for many years, there was no way to link computers together to allow the sharing of information among them. Over the second half of the 1900s, the emergence of the Internet became one of the most important breakthroughs in the history of communication.

38 In the 1960s, the United States government's Department of Defense developed a network (interconnected system) of military and government computers. The network was intended to protect the information on those computers in case of a war or disaster. Soon, universities, corporations, and other organizations developed their own computer networks. Eventually, these networks joined with the government network to form the Internet. The word *Internet* means an interconnected network of networks.

39   The wider application, or use, of the Internet began in 1991. That year, a British computer scientist named Tim Berners-Lee developed the World Wide Web. The Web is made up of electronic addresses called Web sites, which contain Web pages that hold information. People can use the Web to access, or get to, an enormous range of documents, illustrations, sounds, and moving pictures. In many ways, the Web resembles a vast library of interconnected information. Programs called search engines help people sort through this huge amount of information to find what they want.

High-speed cables, cellular towers, and satellites can be used to connect a computer to the Internet.

40   The Internet enables users of computers and similar devices to send and receive messages called e-mail, or electronic mail. Many people communicate over the Internet using instant messaging (IM). This feature enables two people to communicate through text messages that can be seen by both users as the messages are typed.

People can also see and speak to one another through microphones and cameras that are connected to the Internet.

41   New technologies continue to change the way people use the Internet. Handheld computers, cellular telephones, and tablets enable users to access the Internet from almost any location.

The **History of Communication**
Illustrations by Danny Schlitz

Collaborative Discussion

Look back at what you wrote on page 302. Tell a partner two things you learned from this text. Then work with a group to discuss the questions below. Refer to details and examples in *The History of Communication* to explain your answers. Take notes for your responses. When you speak, use your notes.

1 Reread pages 304–305. What does the growth of the printing business tell you about people's interests at the time?

 Listening Tip

Listen carefully as you wait for your turn to speak. Think about questions you may need to ask to better understand what a classmate has said.

2 Review pages 310–311. What features made radio an improvement over the telephone and the telegraph?

 Speaking Tip

Make sure that your comments relate to the question the group is discussing. Save your ideas about other topics until another time.

3 Which of the inventions are based on an earlier invention?

Write a Response

Write a Response

PROMPT ·

Respond to the Text In *The History of Communication,* you learned how inventions over time made communication faster and more effective. Think about how communication has changed over the years. What was the earliest form of communication? What inventions made it easy to communicate across long distances? Cite evidence from the text to support your response.

EVIDENCE ·

List ideas from *The History of Communication* that describe the development of communication over time and the inventions that improved communication.

WRITE

Now write your response in a paragraph.

✓ **Make sure your response**

- ☐ answers the questions.
- ☐ describes the different forms of communication.
- ☐ tells about the inventions that made it possible to communicate over long distances.
- ☐ uses evidence from the text.
- ☐ is written in complete sentences.

myNotes

Notice & Note
3 Big Questions

Prepare to Read

GENRE STUDY **Narrative nonfiction** gives factual information by telling a true story.

- Authors of narrative nonfiction may organize their ideas using headings and subheadings.

- Texts about events that happened in the past include real people and may include how they felt about events.

- Authors of narrative nonfiction may present their ideas in chronological order.

SET A PURPOSE **Think about** the title and genre of this text. What do you know about how people who are hearing impaired communicate? What do you want to learn? Write your ideas below.

Build Background:
Sign Language

CRITICAL VOCABULARY

astonishment

gestures

linguists

instinct

A New Language— Invented by Kids!

by Charnan Simon

1 It sounds like a fairy tale. Once upon a time, in a faraway country, there lived children who could neither hear nor speak.

2 Their lives were lonely, even in the midst of loving families. But one day an amazing thing happened. The silent children, as they were known, were brought together at a new school. They began to make signs with their hands. Faster and faster their hands flew.

3 As the grownups watched in **astonishment**, a new language was born.

The Silent Children

4 The best part about this fairy tale is that it's true. For many years, children who are deaf in the Latin American country of Nicaragua were kept hidden. They were not taught sign language or lipreading or how to write. They were truly children without language.

5 Then, in 1979, the Nicaraguan government set up two schools for them. When the children arrived, they couldn't understand their teachers.

Instead, the children began to "talk" to each other with their hands. At first they shared just simple gestures. But soon they invented more and more signals, until they had their own gesture language.

astonishment If you look at something with astonishment, you feel very surprised by it.

gestures If you make gestures, you make movements with your hands or arms to share a message.

In Our Own Words

6   Their early signing was pretty basic, like baby talk. But as new students arrived at the school, younger children learned from older students and added new signs of their own. The language became richer and more complex. Instead of speaking like two-year-olds and saying, for instance, "I go play," children with more signs could speak fluently—"OK, with Eduardo and Julia, we have enough kids to play soccer. If we hurry, we'll have time for a game before school starts."

7   Can you imagine inventing all the sign language you'd need to say all that?

8   Linguists from around the world were excited about what these Nicaraguan children had done. The children seemed to prove that humans have a natural instinct for language. But unless it is used, this instinct fades away and is eventually lost. For most of us, simply growing up surrounded by people speaking is enough to trigger language learning. For the Nicaraguan children, the trigger seemed to be meeting other children who spoke with hand gestures and who were eager to make friends.

9   Today, Nicaraguan Sign Language is an officially recognized language. It is unlike any other sign language in the world—and it was created entirely by deaf children.

Now that's a happy ending.

linguists   Linguists are people who study languages and the way they are put together.

instinct   An instinct is something you do or know naturally, without being taught.

At the Escuelita de Bluefields ("Little School of Bluefields") in Nicaragua, students who are deaf and teachers communicate in a sign language invented by Nicaraguan children. In class and on the playground, these students use Nicaraguan Sign Language to share news and ideas. Written on the blackboard in SignWriting is their geography lessons. SignWriting is an alphabet used around the world to write down sign languages.

Collaborative Discussion

Look back at what you wrote on page 322. Tell a partner two things you learned from this text. Then work with a group to discuss the questions below. Refer to details and examples in *A New Language—Invented by Kids!* to support your ideas. Take notes for your responses. When you speak, use your notes.

1 Reread page 324. Why does the author say that Nicaraguan children who were deaf were "without language"?

Listening Tip

Listen carefully to what others have to say. Wait until another speaker has finished talking before you add your own ideas.

2 Review page 325. What did the children do to invent a new language?

Speaking Tip

Don't do all the talking! If you've already shared an idea, wait for someone else to speak up before you share again.

3 How did the new language change the lives of the students?

327

Write a Response

PROMPT ....

Respond to the Text In *A New Language—Invented by Kids!*, you read about how children who could not hear or speak found a way to communicate with each other. How did the children develop this system? Cite evidence from the text to support your response. Try to use some of the Critical Vocabulary words in your writing.

EVIDENCE ....

List ideas from *A New Language—Invented by Kids!* that describe how the children developed a way to communicate with each other.

Now write your response in a paragraph.

Make sure your response

- ☐ answers the question.
- ☐ describes how the children learned to communicate with each other.
- ☐ explains how the children developed this form of communication.
- ☐ uses evidence from the text.
- ☐ is written in complete sentences.

Prepare to View

> GENRE STUDY **Informational videos** present facts and information about a topic in visual and audio form.

- A narrator explains what is happening on the screen.
- Science videos may include clips of animals in the wild to illustrate the topic.
- Producers of videos may include sound effects or music in the background to make the video more interesting for viewers.

> SET A PURPOSE **As you watch,** pay attention to the ways in which dolphins communicate to work together. What do you want to learn about how they communicate with one another? Write your ideas below.

**Build Background:
Animal Communication**

CRITICAL VOCABULARY

practical

operation

immaculate

Dolphin Dinner

from National Geographic Kids

▶

As you watch *Dolphin Dinner*, think about the narrator's main purpose. How does the narrator introduce how dolphins communicate with each other? How is that information supported through the visuals? Do the visuals and music make the video more interesting? Why or why not? Take notes in the space below.

Listen for the Critical Vocabulary words *practical*, *operation*, and *immaculate* for clues to the meaning of each word. Take notes in the space below about how the words were used.

practical   If something is practical, it has a useful purpose.

operation   An operation is a set of actions that are carried out to meet a goal.

immaculate   Something that is immaculate has no mistakes or faults.

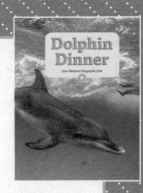

Dolphin Dinner
from National Geographic Kids

Collaborative Discussion

Look back at what you wrote on page 330. Tell a partner something you learned from this video. Then work with a group to discuss the questions below. Support your answers with details and examples from *Dolphin Dinner*. During the discussion, be sure you are sharing your ideas in a way that everyone can understand.

1. How do dusky dolphins use teamwork to get food for their dinner?

2. Why do dolphins send signals to one another? How do they do that?

3. What other animal likes the same kind of food as dolphins?

Listening Tip

Listen closely to what others say about your comments. If they didn't understand something, think of another way to say it, or add details to make your ideas clearer.

Speaking Tip

Use complete sentences and correct grammar when you speak. Include some science words from the video to help your listeners.

Respond to the Video

Write a Response

PROMPT ....

Respond to the Video *Dolphin Dinner* showed how dolphins communicate and work together. Think about the way dolphins communicated with each other. How did they work together to find food? Cite evidence from the video to support your response.

EVIDENCE ....

List ideas from *Dolphin Dinner* that describe how the dolphins used communication to find food.

WRITE ·

Now write your response in a paragraph.

✓	Make sure your response
☐	answers the question.
☐	describes how the dolphins communicated with each other.
☐	explains how the dolphins worked together to find food.
☐	uses evidence from the video.
☐	is written in complete sentences.

Notice & Note
Aha Moment

Prepare to Read

GENRE STUDY **Realistic fiction** tells a story about characters and events that are like those in real life.

- Authors of realistic fiction tell the story through the plot—the main events of the story.

- Characters in realistic fiction might tell an anecdote. An anecdote may be told when the author wants to introduce an event that happened in a character's past.

- Some realistic fiction includes a theme or lesson learned by the main character.

SET A PURPOSE **Look at** the pictures in this text. What do you notice about the main character? What would you like to learn about him? Write your ideas below.

Meet the Author:
Sun Yung Shin

CRITICAL VOCABULARY

inspect

liveliest

stammered

expectantly

demonstrated

Cooper's Lesson

story by **Sun Yung Shin**

illustrated by **Kim Cogan**

1 Cooper's pocket felt heavy with his allowance. He leashed his dog, Catso, and laced his shoes.

2 "Be home by dinnertime!" called Cooper's dad.

3 "Cooper!" exclaimed his mom. "Could you pick up some ginger at Mr. Lee's store? *Kamsahamnida!*"

4 Cooper sighed. His mom always insisted on speaking only Korean to Mr. Lee, even though Cooper could barely follow along. Once, Mr. Lee had scolded him—in Korean—for not speaking Korean. Since then, Cooper felt funny every time he walked past the old man's store.

5 "Sure, Mom!" Cooper called over his shoulder, as he and Catso began their walk through the neighborhood.

6 A poster hung in the window of Mr. Lee's grocery store for a new Tae Kwon Do gym in the neighborhood. Both kids on the poster had black hair and yellow-brown skin.

7 Cooper studied his reflection in the window. Brown hair and some freckles. Grandmother Park always said, "Such white skin!" and Grandmother Daly always said, "What brown skin!" One cousin always teased him about being "half and half."

8 Cooper frowned. In the window, the stacked packages of powdered *insam* and bars of soap wrapped in red-and-white paper made a perfect miniature skyline.

9 He tied Catso's leash to a No Parking sign and went inside.

10 Inside, families filled the aisles, laughing and smiling. Mothers picked up vegetables to carefully inspect their leaves and roots, or gently squeezed round, sweet melons. Fathers examined the fish in the tank, searching out the largest and liveliest.

> **inspect**   If you inspect something, you look at it carefully to judge its quality.
>
> **liveliest**   The liveliest person or animal is the one that is the most active or full of energy.

11   Cooper's ears were buzzing. He realized he had never been inside without his mother. *Everyone seems to belong here,* he thought.

12   One woman with a small, sleeping boy in her arms smiled at Cooper and said, "*An yong.*"

13   "Hello," Cooper stammered, blushing.

14   "*An yong ha se oh,*" he added quietly, but she was already out the door.

15   Cooper wandered past the boxes of green tea and packages of shrimp crackers, and stopped at a display of hairbrushes and barrettes.

16   Cooper remembered. The week before, he had gone outside to brush Catso. He had grabbed the first brush he could find—his mother's—and spent the next half-hour brushing Catso's coat to a glossy shine.

> **stammered**   If you stammered, you spoke with many pauses and repeated words.

17   The next morning, when Cooper left for school, his mother found her brush on the table in the hallway, full of Catso's brown and white fur.

18   "Cooper! My brush! Ruined!" cried his mom.

19   *I know—I'll buy her a new one with my allowance!* Cooper smiled to himself.

20   But Cooper's heart sank—even the smallest brush on display cost more than the three dollars in his pocket.

21   Mr. Lee called out to him from the register, but Mr. Lee's Korean was too quick for Cooper to catch.

22   Mr. Lee walked over to Cooper. *Is he laughing at me?* Cooper wondered. He wanted to answer back in Korean, English, anything, but his tongue lay as heavy and still in his mouth as a dead fish.

23   He was sorry that he had paid so little attention when his mother had tried to teach him Korean. Mr. Lee watched him expectantly.

expectantly   If you do something expectantly, you are excited that something good is about to happen.

341

24   "Uh . . . is this all you have?" Cooper finally squeaked out.

25   Mr. Lee frowned and said, "*Ye. Mullon imnida?*" When Cooper didn't answer, Mr. Lee shook his head and walked away.

26   The Korean writing on the cans and boxes seemed to dance off the labels. The aisles were closing in on him from all sides.

27   Cooper felt the money in his pocket. *Dumb, small allowance!*

28   He looked at Mr. Lee and thought to himself, *Why don't you speak English to me?* Cooper felt hot prickles under his skin.

29   Suddenly, Cooper's hand reached out and grabbed the biggest brush from the rack. As though in a dream, he turned and moved toward the door.

30   He was halfway outside when a firm hand gripped his shoulder.

31   "What do you have there?"

32   "Nothing," stammered Cooper, his eyes open wide. Since when could Mr. Lee speak English?

33   Mr. Lee took the brush from Cooper's hand.

34   "It—it was for my mother!"

35   Mr. Lee bent down to look at Cooper. "Would your mother want you to steal for her? Is that what she teaches you?"

36   "No . . ." said Cooper, blushing red to his ears.

37   "Any other 'nothings' in your pocket?" asked Mr. Lee. Cooper pulled his allowance from his pocket. Mr. Lee shook his head in disbelief. "Come with me," he sighed.

38   Mr. Lee handed Cooper a broom. "Do you know how to use one of these?" he asked. Cooper nodded, his voice nowhere to be found. He had never felt so ashamed in his entire life.

39   So Cooper swept. And swept. And swept some more.

40   After sweeping the day's dust into the trash bin, Cooper went and stood in front of Mr. Lee, unsure of what to say or do.

41   "Come back tomorrow, same time," said Mr. Lee, with a look that told Cooper he'd better return.

42   Cooper's stomach hurt as he thought about what to tell his mother. Would Mr. Lee call her before he got home?

43   Cooper closed the front door quietly behind him, but not quietly enough.

44   "Oh good, you're back! Cooper, we need that ginger, quick!" his mom called from the kitchen.

45   Visions of the afternoon—his too-small allowance, the hairbrush, the broom—flashed before him. "Oh no," he groaned, his chin dropping to his chest.

46   "You forgot? *Aigo!* What were you doing all this time?" asked his mom. Cooper wanted to apologize, but she had gone back to cooking. Once again, his tongue failed him. He would tell her about Mr. Lee and the hairbrush tomorrow.

47   The next day after school, Cooper dragged his feet to Mr. Lee's store.

48   Mr. Lee demonstrated how to place cans on the shelves so that the labels lined up perfectly. He spoke to Cooper first in Korean and then in English. Cooper tried it. Mr. Lee nodded silently, then walked away.

49   After he had placed the last can on the shelf, Cooper watched Mr. Lee chat with his customers at the register. Cooper realized suddenly that sometimes, if he paid very close attention, he could understand what they said.

50   On his way home, Cooper passed a leafy oak tree. *Namu.* The Korean word for *tree* rose in his mind, surprising him, like a fish breaking the surface of a calm pond.

---

demonstrated   If you demonstrated something, you showed how it is used or done.

51   By the end of the week, Cooper's feet no longer dragged as he walked to Mr. Lee's. He even caught himself whistling as he swept.

52   Mr. Lee approached. His tired face was gentle. He bent down to look Cooper in the eye and said, "So. Are you ready to tell me why you stole from me?"

53   "I don't know!" Cooper said, although then he felt that perhaps he did know. "I'm sorry. I thought you were laughing at me because I couldn't speak Korean. I got mad."

54   "I know how that feels, believe it or not," said Mr. Lee, "but stealing is still wrong."

55   "I know," said Cooper, his voice small.

56   "Oh good," said Mr. Lee. "Maybe there's hope for you yet."

57   Suddenly Mr. Lee motioned for Cooper to follow him to the register. He pulled a slim photo album from beneath the counter and opened it to a photo of a young man in a white coat next to a modern-looking building. The sign over the door was in bold Korean lettering.

58   Cooper's eyes widened. "Is that you?"

59   Mr. Lee nodded. "When I was a chemist in Korea, I had the neatest lab in the company."

60   "You were a chemist?"

61   "Yes. But when I came here, I had to start over with a new language."

62   "But English is easy!" Cooper blurted.

63   Mr. Lee laughed. "Yes . . . About as easy as Korean."
Cooper blushed.

64   "Anyway, now I speak both. And now that I'm a citizen, I'm Korean and American, both."

65   "I guess I'm both too, but people ask me where I'm from all the time," said Cooper.

66   "What do you tell them?" asked Mr. Lee.

67   "That I'm from right here. But then they say, *No, where are your parents from?* Sometimes I feel like I can't really say I'm Korean if I can't speak the language. But they look at me funny if I say I'm American, even though I am." Cooper glanced back at the photo album. He wondered if people looked at Mr. Lee funny for saying he was Korean and American, too.

68   "People like things to be simple, easy to put in a box," sighed Mr. Lee.

69   "Sometimes I wish I were just one thing or another. It *would* be simpler," Cooper said.

70   "Oh? You want to be the same as everyone else, like the cans on this shelf, or those rows of frozen fish?"

71   Cooper wrinkled his nose. The bell on the door jingled. "There you are!" said a voice from behind Cooper.

72   "Mom! I was . . . here to get the ginger. I mean, *saenggang*," said Cooper, choosing a thick piece and fishing in his pocket for a dollar bill.

73   Cooper's mother looked surprised. Then she smiled and said, "Well, better late than never."

74   Cooper's mother turned to Mr. Lee and spoke in Korean.

75   Mr. Lee began to close the store. In English, he replied, "Thank you, I would be honored to join you for dinner. And perhaps on the way home Cooper can tell you why he's been here so much lately. Right, Cooper?" said Mr. Lee.

76   Cooper looked at his mom's curious face. He suddenly felt more grown-up than he ever had before.

77   They left the store and Cooper began, *"Igosul Hanguk-o-ro mworago malhamnikka?"*—*How do you say this in Korean?* Cooper's Korean felt awkward and funny in his own ears, but he worked hard to say exactly what he meant.

78   His mom looked at him, even more surprised. "Well, tell me what it is and we'll figure it out together," she said. Mr. Lee nodded.

79   The sun dipped behind them as they walked along, the soft sound of their languages mingling in the gentle evening air.

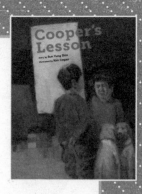

Collaborative Discussion

Look back at what you wrote on page 336. Tell a partner two things you learned about Cooper. Then work with a group to discuss the questions below. Use details and examples from *Cooper's Lesson* when you explain your answers. Take notes for your responses. When you speak, use your notes.

1   Review pages 339–340. Why does Cooper feel out of place in Mr. Lee's store?

 Listening Tip

Pay close attention to what each speaker says. Then try to think of new details on the same topic that come from the text.

2   Reread pages 341–342. What details in the text show why Cooper decided to take the hair brush?

Speaking Tip

Link the ideas that you share with the comments already made by other group members.

3   What does Cooper learn from Mr. Lee?

Write a Response

PROMPT ....

Respond to the Text In *Cooper's Lesson*, you read about a boy who learned a lesson and made a new friend. Think about how being unable to understand Mr. Lee made Cooper feel. How did Cooper respond to this language barrier? What lesson did he learn?

EVIDENCE ....

List ideas from *Cooper's Lesson* that describe how Cooper learned a lesson.

WRITE

Now write your response in a paragraph.

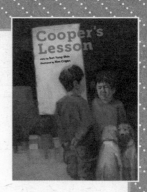

✓	Make sure your response
☐	answers the questions.
☐	explains how Cooper felt when he didn't understand Mr. Lee.
☐	explains the lesson that Cooper learned and how he learned it.
☐	uses evidence from the text.
☐	is written in complete sentences.

Essential Question

What forms can communication take?

Write an Expository Essay

PROMPT Think about the forms of communication you read about in this module. In what ways do people and animals communicate? Choose three forms of communication from what you read. Write an expository essay about why those three forms of communication are important. Use evidence, facts, and examples from the texts and the video to support your ideas. Use some of the module vocabulary words in your essay.

✓ Make sure your expository essay

☐ introduces your topic.

☐ describes three different forms of communication.

☐ uses text evidence to support ideas.

☐ uses details to elaborate.

☐ provides a conclusion.

Think about the different forms of communication you learned about in this module. Why is each one important? Complete the map below using the following sentence frame in each bubble: _____ is an important form of communication because _____.

Forms of Communication

DRAFT ·· Write your expository essay.

Use the information you wrote on page 355 to draft your expository essay. Write a **beginning paragraph** that **introduces** your topic.

⬇

Choose your three strongest sentences from page 355. Write **body paragraphs** that tell about three different forms of communication and why they are important. Use details to elaborate.

⬇

Write a **conclusion** that summarizes your ideas.

The revision and editing steps give you a chance to look carefully at your draft and make changes. Work with a partner to determine whether you have clearly supported your topic and explained your ideas. Use these questions to help you.

✓ PURPOSE/ FOCUS	ORGANIZATION	EVIDENCE/SUPPORT	ELABORATION	CONVENTIONS
☐ Does my essay answer all the questions? ☐ Did I explain three different forms of communication and why they are important?	☐ Do I have a clear introduction to my topic? ☐ Does my conclusion summarize my topic?	☐ Did I include text evidence and examples from the selections?	☐ Did I use details to elaborate? ☐ Did I use any module vocabulary words?	☐ Have I used correct punctuation and capitalization? ☐ Did I indent each new paragraph?

PUBLISH ⋯⋯⋯⋯⋯⋯⋯⋯⋯⋯⋯⋯⋯⋯⋯ Create a finished copy.

Make a final copy of your expository essay. Write legibly using your cursive writing skills.

Glossary

This glossary contains meanings and pronunciations for some of the words in this book. The Full Pronunciation Key shows how to pronounce each consonant and vowel in a special spelling. At the bottom of the glossary pages is a shortened form of the full key.

Full Pronunciation Key

CONSONANT SOUNDS

b	**b**i**b**, ca**bb**age	s	mi**ss**, **s**auce,
ch	**ch**ur**ch**, sti**tch**		**sc**ene, **s**ee
d	**d**ee**d**, maile**d**,	sh	di**sh**, **sh**ip, **s**ugar,
	pu**dd**le		ti**ss**ue
f	**f**ast, **f**i**f**e, o**ff**,	t	**t**igh**t**, stopp**ed**
	phrase, rou**gh**	th	ba**th**, **th**in
g	**g**a**g**, **g**et, fin**g**er	*th*	ba**th**e, **th**is
h	**h**at, w**h**o	v	ca**v**e, **v**al**v**e, **v**ine
hw	**wh**ich, **wh**ere	w	**w**ith, **w**olf
j	**j**u**dg**e, **g**em	y	**y**es, **y**olk, on**i**on
k	**c**at, **k**i**ck**, s**ch**ool	z	ro**s**e, si**z**e,
kw	**ch**oir, **qu**ick		**x**ylophone, **z**ebra
l	**l**id, need**l**e, ta**ll**	zh	gara**g**e, plea**s**ure,
m	a**m**, **m**an, du**mb**		vi**s**ion
n	**n**o, sudd**en**		
ng	thi**ng**, i**nk**		
p	**p**op, ha**pp**y		
r	**r**oar, **rh**yme		

VOWEL SOUNDS

ă	p**a**t, l**au**gh	o͝o	f**u**ll, b**oo**k, w**o**lf
ā	**a**pe, **ai**d, p**ay**	o͞o	b**oo**t, r**u**de, fr**ui**t,
â	**ai**r, c**a**re, w**ea**r		fl**ew**
ä	f**a**ther, k**oa**la, y**a**rd	ŭ	c**u**t, fl**oo**d, r**ou**gh,
ĕ	p**e**t, pl**ea**sure, **a**ny		s**o**me
ē	b**e**, b**ee**, **ea**sy,	û	c**i**rcle, f**u**r, h**ea**rd,
	p**i**ano		t**e**rm, t**u**rn, **u**rge,
ĭ	**i**f, p**i**t, b**u**sy		w**o**rd
ī	r**i**de, b**y**, p**ie**, h**igh**	yo͞o	c**u**re
î	d**ea**r, d**ee**r, f**ie**rce,	yo͞o	ab**u**se, **u**se
	m**e**re	ə	**a**go, sil**e**nt, penc**i**l,
ŏ	h**o**rrible, p**o**t		lem**o**n, circ**u**s
ō	g**o**, r**o**w, t**oe**,		
	th**ough**		
ô	**a**ll, c**au**ght, f**o**r,		
	p**aw**		
oi	b**oy**, n**oi**se, **oi**l		
ou	c**ow**, **ou**t		

STRESS MARKS

Primary Stress ´: biology [bī·**ŏl**´·ə·jē]

Secondary Stress ´: biological [bī´·ə·**lŏj**´·ĭ·kəl]

abandoned

autonomous

A

abandoned (ə•**băn'**•dənd) *adj.* If a place is abandoned, it is no longer cared for or used. There is an abandoned car left in the field.

accentuated (ăk•**sĕn'**•chōō•ā'•tĭd) *v.* If something is accentuated, it has attention drawn to it. She accentuated her pigtails by wearing pink hair bands.

adventurous (əd•**vĕn'**•chər•əs) *adj.* Someone who is adventurous tries to do new things. The adventurous family was excited about their bike ride up the mountain.

ancestors (**ăn'**•sĕs'•tərz) *n.* Your ancestors are the people in your family who lived long ago. My grandfather told me that my ancestors came from several countries on the continent of Europe over one hundred years ago.

Word Origins

ancestors The word *ancestors* comes from the Latin word *antecedere*. The prefix *ante-* means "before" or "to precede." Thus the meaning of *ancestors* came to be "the people in your family who came before you."

---

appointed (ə•**poin'**•tĭd) *v.* If you are appointed to a job, you are assigned to or chosen for it. Kaito was appointed as the caretaker for the classroom plants.

assess (ə•**sĕs'**) *v.* If you assess something, you think about it carefully and judge it. On the way to school, we stopped to assess the safety of the street before crossing.

assumed (ə•**sōōmd'**) *v.* If you assumed something, you believed it without proof. When Matthew went to bed, Mom assumed that he would stop reading and go to sleep.

astonishment (ə•**stŏn'**•ĭsh•mənt) *n.* If you look at something with astonishment, you feel very surprised by it. Penny had a look of astonishment when she saw what was inside the box.

astounded (ə•**stoun'**•dĭd) *v.* If you are astounded by something, you are completely surprised by it. We were astounded by the show on TV.

attitudes (**ăt'**•ĭ•tōōdz') *n.* Your attitudes are the ways you think and feel about something. The coach gives our team a pep talk to help us keep positive attitudes as we play the game.

autonomous (ô•**tŏn'**•ə•məs) *adj.* If something is autonomous, it controls itself. The autonomous machines in the factory are assembling cars.

ōō b**oo**t / ou **ou**t / ŭ c**u**t / û f**u**r / hw **wh**ich / th **th**in / *th* **th**is / zh vi**si**on / ə **a**go, sil**e**nt, penc**i**l, lem**o**n, circ**u**s

B

blog (blŏg) *n.* If you write a blog, you are writing regular and informal updates, or entries, on a website. The students created a blog about how to care for a community garden.

blunt (blŭnt) *adj.* Something that is blunt is flat or rounded, rather than sharp. The blunt pencil still needs to be sharpened.

broadcast (brôd'•kăst') *n.* A broadcast is a program or speech on the television or radio. Robert listened to the radio broadcast of the concert.

C

canopy (kăn'•ə•pē) *n.* A canopy is a rooflike covering, like the top branches of trees in a forest. A canopy of trees shades the dirt road.

canyon (kăn'•yən) *n.* A canyon is a deep valley that has steep sides. He felt dizzy as he looked down into the canyon.

character (kăr'•ĭk•tər) *n.* A person's character is the kind of person he or she is. Peter has an outgoing character, as he is easily able to talk to anyone he meets.

chasm (kăz'•əm) *n.* A chasm is a deep crack or opening in the ground. The hikers enjoy the beauty created by the chasm.

clamped (klămpt) *v.* When something is clamped, it is closed tightly. The puppy clamped its teeth tightly onto the tasty bone.

collision (kə•lĭzh'•ən) *n.* A collision happens when a moving object crashes into something. Rubber bumpers softened the collision between bumper cars.

commendable (kə•mĕnd'•a•bəl) *adj.* If you do something commendable, you do it well and earn praise. The officer received many medals for his commendable service in the military.

compost (kŏm'•pōst') *n.* Compost is decayed plant waste that can be used to fertilize soil. The compost we make will be used in our vegetable garden.

conservation (kŏn'•sər•vā'•shən) *n.* Conservation is the act of saving and protecting the environment. People are working hard for the conservation of wildlife in this area.

convenient (kən•vēn'•yənt) *adj.* If something is convenient, it is handy and useful. My dad takes the train because it is the most convenient way for him to get to work.

core (kôr) *n.* The core of something is its center. Daniel ate every bite of the delicious apple and left only the core.

correspond (kôr'•ĭ•spŏnd') *v.* When you correspond with someone, you exchange letters or emails with that person. The class was assigned to correspond with their pen pals for the entire school year.

ă r**a**t / ā p**ay** / â c**a**re / ä f**a**ther / ĕ p**e**t / ē b**e** / ĭ p**i**t / ī p**ie** / î f**ie**rce / ŏ p**o**t / ō g**o** / ô p**aw** / ôr f**or** / oi **oi**l / o͝o b**oo**k /

crestfallen (**krĕst'**•fô'•lən) *adj.* If you are crestfallen, you are sad and discouraged. When his team lost the final game of the season, Zack was crestfallen.

culinary (**kŭl'**•ə•nĕr'•ē) *adj.* Something that is culinary is connected to cooking. Jackie plans to go to culinary school when she gets older because she really enjoys cooking.

currents (**kûr'**•əntz) *n.* Currents are flowing movements of water in a lake, river, or ocean. The strong water currents quickly move the kayak down the river.

D

decay (dĭ•**kā'**) *v.* When things decay, they slowly break down and rot. The apple looked like it was brown and starting to decay.

demonstrated (**dĕm'**•ən•strā'•tĭd) *v.* If you demonstrated something, you showed how it is used or done. The ballet instructor demonstrated the pose to the students.

devastation (**dĕv'**•ə•stā'•shən) *n.* Devastation is terrible damage or complete destruction. Many buildings were destroyed due to the devastation caused by the tornado.

digest (dĭ•**jĕst'**) *v.* When you digest food, it moves through your body to your stomach. Some foods, like meats and cheese, take longer to digest than others.

disoriented (dĭs•**ôr'**•ē•ĕn'•tĭd) *v.* Creatures that are disoriented are confused about where they are. The tourist was disoriented and needed to look at a map.

disposable (dĭ•**spō'**•zə•bəl) *adj.* If something is disposable, it is meant to be thrown away once it has been used. The trashcan was overflowing with disposable cardboard boxes and wrappers.

disposition (dĭs'•pə•**zĭsh'**•ən) *n.* Your disposition is the way you tend to act or feel. I really enjoy spending time with my friend Juanita because she has such a happy disposition.

diverse (dĭ•**vûrs'**) *adj.* If something is diverse, it is made up of things that are different from each other. The marine life in the ocean is so diverse that I saw over forty types of fish at the aquarium.

E

ecology (ĭ•**kŏl'**•ə•jē) *n.* Ecology is the relationship between the living things in their environment. I wrote about the ecology of the rainforest for my science project.

edible (**ĕd'**•ə•bəl) *adj.* If something is edible, it is safe for people to eat. Some flowers are edible.

> **Word Origins**
>
> **edible** The word *edible* comes from the Latin word *edere*, which means "to eat."

embedded (ĕm•**bĕ'**•dĭd) *v.* If a thing is embedded, it is firmly set into something else that surrounds it. An oyster will create a pearl when a grain of sand becomes embedded in the soft tissue within its shell.

ōō b**oo**t / ou **ou**t / ŭ c**u**t / û f**u**r / hw **wh**ich / th **th**in / *th* **th**is / zh vi**si**on / ə **a**go, sil**e**nt, penc**i**l, lem**o**n, circ**u**s

enabled (ĕn·**ā'**·bəld) v. If you are enabled to do something, you are given a chance to do it. The crutches enabled Darla to walk with her hurt leg.

envision (ĕn·**vĭzh'**·ən) v. If you envision something, you picture it in your mind. Charlotte likes to envision herself becoming an astronaut in the future.

eroding (ĭ·**rōd'**·ĭng) v. If something is eroding, it is slowly wearing away, often from wind or water. The rocks have been eroding for years as a result of the daily rush of water.

estimate (ĕs'·tə·mĭt) n. If you give an estimate, you give an amount or size that is not exact. Our teacher taught us that finding an estimate first can be a helpful step when solving a math problem.

eternal (ĭ·**tûr'**·nəl) adj. If something is eternal, it has no end and lasts forever. There is an eternal flame at Arlington National Cemetery.

Word Origins

eternal The word *eternal* comes from the Latin word *aeternus*, which means "age."

---

exaggeration (ĭg·zăj'·ə·**rā'**·shən) n. An exaggeration describes something as more important or larger than what it really is. Saying that your sister is twice as tall as you are is an exaggeration.

expectantly (ĭk·**spĕk'**·tənt·lē) adv. If you do something expectantly, you are excited that something good is about to happen. Gregory looks in the box expectantly, eager to see what is inside.

F

fascinated (**făs'**·ə·nā'·tĭd) v. If you are fascinated by something, you are very interested in it. Ella is fascinated with searching for places on the globe.

fathom (**fă***th***'**·əm) v. If you fathom something, you understand it. Roberto could not fathom how the goat got stuck in the fence.

forbidden (fər·**bĭd'**·n) adj. If something is forbidden, it is not allowed or accepted. My little sister sneaks into my mom's room and uses her makeup, even though she knows that it is forbidden.

frequent (**frē'**·kwənt) adj. If something is frequent, it happens often. I take frequent trips overseas.

G

generous (**jĕn'**·ər·əs) adj. A generous amount of something is larger or more plentiful than is usual or necessary. I was amazed by the generous number of gifts at my birthday party.

gestures (**jĕs'**·chərz) n. If you make gestures, you make movements with your hands or arms to share a message. As my teacher talks, she makes a lot of gestures with her hands.

glimpse (glĭmps) n. A glimpse is a very quick look at something. We saw a glimpse of two orcas as they surfaced.

ă r**a**t / ā p**ay** / â c**a**re / ä f**a**ther / ĕ p**e**t / ē b**e** / ĭ p**i**t / ī p**ie** / î f**ie**rce / ŏ p**o**t / ō g**o** / ô p**aw** / ôr f**or** / oi **oi**l / oͦo b**oo**k /

glistens (**glĭs′**•ənz) *v.* If something glistens, it sparkles or shines. The dew-covered spider web glistens in the early morning sunshine.

gratitude (**grăt′**•ĭ•tōōd′) *n.* When you show gratitude, you show that you are thankful. Theresa shows her gratitude by giving her mom a big hug.

H

hydrated (**hī′**•drā′•tĭd) *v.* Something that is hydrated has taken in plenty of water. The players are given water before, during, and after the game so they stay hydrated.

I

idle (**īd′**•l) *adj.* If something is referred to as idle, it is not doing anything. An idle boast is bragging about something that cannot happen. Sloths spend much of their time being idle in the treetops.

immaculate (ĭ•**măk′**•yə•lĭt) *adj.* Something that is immaculate has no mistakes or faults. Benji's performance is immaculate and precise.

impact (**ĭm′**•păkt) *n.* Impact is the effect that one thing has on something else. The heavy snow makes an impact on our travel plans.

influence (**ĭn′**•flōō•əns) *v.* If you influence people, you use your power or ability to change what they think. Daria's teacher was able to influence her to play the clarinet.

inspect (ĭn•**spĕkt′**) *v.* If you inspect something, you look at it carefully to judge its quality. To ensure the safety of the children at our school, an official came to inspect all of the fire extinguishers and alarms.

installing (ĭn•**stôl′**•lĭng) *v.* If you are installing something, you are setting it up so it is ready to use. He is carefully installing a stained glass window.

instinct (**ĭn′**•stĭngkt′) *n.* An instinct is something you do or know naturally, without being taught. Most animals, including humans, are born with the instinct to do whatever is necessary to survive, such as eating.

intensive (ĭn•**tĕn′**•sĭv) *adj.* Something that is intensive uses a lot of effort to complete a task. We know it is an intensive task to clean up the backyard.

intriguing (ĭn•**trē′**•gĭng) *adj.* Something that is intriguing is very interesting. Isabelle thinks that space is intriguing and hopes to be an astronaut one day.

L

landform (**lănd′**•fôrm′) *n.* A landform is a natural feature, such as a mountain, of a land's surface. The tallest landform in the world is Mount Everest.

ōō b**oo**t / ou **ou**t / ŭ c**u**t / û f**u**r / hw **wh**ich / th **th**in / *th* **th**is / zh vi**s**ion / ə **a**go, sil**e**nt, penc**i**l, lem**o**n, circ**u**s

landscape (**lănd'**•skāp') *n.* When you look at a landscape, you are looking at the area of land around you. The landscape of a forest is thick with trees.

legendary (**lĕj'**•ən•dĕr'•ē) *adj.* If something is legendary, it is very famous and has had many stories told about it. Many people have read the legendary story of Hercules.

linguists (**lĭng'**•gwĭsts) *n.* Linguists are people who study languages and the way they are put together. My aunt and her co-workers are linguists who speak and study many languages.

liveliest (**līv'**•lē•ĭst) *adj.* The liveliest person or animal is the one that is the most active or full of energy. We picked our puppy, Luna, because she was the liveliest one in the litter.

luscious (**lŭsh'**•əs) *adj.* A food that is luscious is tasty and often juicy. Marco and Valentina thoroughly enjoy the sweet taste of the luscious strawberries.

N

nutrition (noō•**trĭsh'**•ən) *n.* If you have good nutrition, you eat the right foods to help you stay healthy and grow. Good nutrition includes eating fresh fruits, vegetables, and lean protein.

O

oasis (ō•**ā'**•sĭs) *n.* An oasis is a relaxing or peaceful spot in an area that is unpleasant in some way. My dad enjoys going to the park because it is an oasis where he can relax.

obsessed (əb•**sĕsd'**) *adj.* If you are obsessed with something, you think about it all the time. My sister is obsessed with taking pictures.

offense (ə•**fĕns'**) *n.* An offense is something that makes you feel hurt, annoyed, or insulted. Our pets think it is a major offense that they have to share the same yard.

── **Word Origins** ──

offense The word *offense* comes from the Latin word *offendere*, which means "strike against."

operation (ŏp'•ə•**rā'**•shən) *n.* An operation is a set of actions that are carried out to meet a goal. My dad is an engineer at a facility where the main operation is to clean the water that will be used in homes around the city.

opted (**ŏp'**•tĭd') *v.* If you opted for something, you chose it. After careful thought, Mason opted to wear a long-sleeved shirt and jeans to school.

organic (ôr•**găn'**•ĭk) *adj.* If something is organic, it is made up of living matter. Soil is made from minerals and organic matter.

ă **ra**t / ā **pay** / â **ca**re / ä **fa**ther / ĕ **pe**t / ē **be** / ĭ **pi**t / ī **pie** / î **fie**rce / ŏ **po**t / ō **go** / ô **paw** / ôr **for** / oi **oil** / ōo **boo**k /

outspoken (out•**spō'**•kən) *adj.* If you are outspoken, you say what you think even when others do not agree. Grace is outspoken and is not afraid to give her opinion.

P

partial (**pär'**•shəl) *adj.* If you are partial to something, you prefer it more than other things. Mom made pasta for dinner because she knew that Nicholas was partial to it.

patent (**păt'**•nt) *n.* If you have a patent for an invention, you are the only one who is allowed to make or sell the invention. My uncle is a lawyer, and he works to help inventors write a patent for their inventions.

peak (pēk) *n.* A peak is the highest point of something. This restaurant's business is at its peak during lunchtime.

permission (pər•**mǐsh'**•ən) *n.* If you get permission, someone who is in charge allows you to do what you asked to do. David asks permission to open his gift.

pests (pĕsts) *n.* Pests are insects or small animals that harm crops or annoy people. There are many pests in the forest.

plucked (plŭkd) *v.* If something is plucked, it is pulled away from where it is. Ana plucked the apple from the highest branch of the tree.

--- **Word Origins** ---

plucked The word *plucked* is from the Old English word *ploccian*, which means "pull off, cull."

practical (**prăk'**•tǐ•kəl) *adj.* If something is practical, it has a useful purpose. My younger brother dressed in a raincoat and boots, which were very practical in this weather.

prehistoric (prē'•hǐ•**stôr'**•ǐk) *adj.* Something that is prehistoric is very old, from a time before history was recorded. Prehistoric animals, like dinosaurs, roamed the Earth long before people.

proposed (prə•**pōzd'**) *v.* If you proposed an idea, you suggested that it was useful or true. Mom proposed that the family go for a bike ride since it was such a beautiful day.

prosper (**prŏs'**•pər) *v.* If you prosper, you succeed and do well. The tree was able to prosper over the years.

publication (pŭb'•lǐ•**kā'**•shən) *n.* A publication is something that has been printed and made available for sale. My favorite publication is a newspaper that contains stories from local authors.

ōō b**oo**t / ou **ou**t / ŭ c**u**t / û f**u**r / hw **wh**ich / th **th**in / *th* **th**is / zh vi**si**on / ə **a**go, sil**e**nt, penc**i**l, lem**o**n, circ**u**s

R

react (rē•**ăkt'**) *v.* When you react to something, you act in a way that shows you are aware of it. The baseball player had to react quickly to tag the runner out.

recall (rĭ•**kôl'**) *v.* If you recall something, you tell about something you remember. Sienna had a look of concentration as she tried to recall the information.

reckless (**rĕk'**•lĭs) *adj.* Someone who is reckless does not care how his or her actions affect others. It is reckless to leave a cord on the ground where someone could trip over it.

recruiting (rĭ•**krōo'**•tĭng) *v.* If you are recruiting people, you are asking them to help do something. Akari began recruiting her friends to help collect canned goods for the food drive.

recycle (rē•**sī'**•kəl) *v.* If you recycle something, you put it through a process so that it can be reused. Remember to recycle the newspaper after you read it.

remotely (rĭ•**mōt'**•lē) *adj.* If you use something remotely, you control it from a distance. The toy car can be controlled remotely.

resourceful (rĭ•**sôrs'**•fəl) *adj.* If you are resourceful, you are good at solving problems quickly. My grandfather is very resourceful because he is able to fix almost anything that is broken.

S

sanctuary (**săngk'**•chŏo•ĕr'•ē) *n.* A sanctuary is where people or animals go to be safe from danger. The elephants are safe living in the animal sanctuary.

scenic (**sē'**•nĭk) *adj.* Something that is scenic has beautiful scenery. The scenic cliffs towered over the beach.

scorching (**skôrch'**•ĭng) *adj.* Something that is scorching is very, very hot. As the volcano erupted, scorching lava flowed down its sides.

sentries (**sĕn'**•trēz) *n.* Sentries are guards or lookouts who stand in a place to keep watch. The palace has sentries standing guard in front of the gates.

shatter (**shăt'**•ər) *v.* When things shatter, they explode or suddenly break into pieces. Grayson saw the window shatter.

shrewd (shrōod) *adj.* Someone who is shrewd is able to quickly understand a situation to gain an advantage. Her shrewd decisions helped us get out of a difficult situation.

significantly (sĭg•**nĭf'**•ĭ•kənt•lē) *adv.* If something changes significantly, the change is great enough to be noticed or important. When Kari practiced for thirty minutes each day during the summer, her playing improved significantly.

ă rat / ā pay / â care / ä father / ĕ pet / ē be / ĭ pit / ī pie / î fierce / ŏ pot / ō go / ô paw / ôr for / oi oil / ŏŏ book /

sneered (snîrd) *v.* If you sneered, you showed disapproval and lack of respect by the look on your face. If someone sneered at you, it might hurt your feelings.

splendor (**splĕn′**•dər) *n.* The splendor of something is its great beauty or impressive appearance. When we walked into the wedding reception, we were amazed by the splendor of the decorations.

stammered (**stăm′**•ərd) *v.* If you stammered, you spoke with many pauses and repeated words. Lilly was so nervous about reciting her poem to the class that she stammered through the first few lines.

stranded (**străn′**•dĭd) *v.* If you are stranded, you are stuck somewhere without a way to leave. Mom is stranded because her car broke down on her way to work.

submersible (səb•**mûr′**•sə•bəl) *adj.* If something is submersible, it can go or work under water. A submersible camera is nice to use when scuba diving.

succulent (**sŭk′**•yə•lənt) *adj.* If food is succulent, it is juicy and tasty. I enjoyed the taste of the succulent watermelon, as the sweet juices ran down my chin.

Word Origins

succulent The word *succulent* comes from the Latin word *succulentus*, which means "juice."

---

sufficient (sə•**fĭsh′**•ənt) *adj.* If something is sufficient, it is just what is needed and no more. The smaller suitcase is sufficient to fit all of Leah's clothes for the weekend.

summit (**sŭm′**•ĭt) *n.* The summit of a mountain is its top or highest point. The summit of the Matterhorn has a unique shape.

sustainable (sə•**stā′**•nə•bəl) *adj.* If you use a natural resource that is sustainable, it is able to stay at a certain level and not cause harm to the environment. Farmers are trying to grow food in a sustainable way.

swirled (swûrld) *v.* If something swirled, it moved quickly around in circles. My mother swirled the cream into her coffee.

T

thrifty (**thrĭf′**•tē) *adj.* If you are thrifty, you save your money and buy only what you need. By being thrifty, Neal was able to save lots of money.

thrive (thrīv) *v.* When living things thrive, they grow well and are healthy. Many types of plants thrive in a rainforest.

ōō b**oo**t / ou **ou**t / ŭ c**u**t / û f**u**r / hw **wh**ich / th **th**in / *th* **th**is / zh vi**s**ion / ə **a**go, sil**e**nt, penc**i**l, lem**o**n, circ**u**s

transmitted (trăns•**mĭ'**•tĭd) *v.* If something is transmitted, it is sent electronically from one place to another. After I finished my book report, I transmitted the assignment to my teacher by email.

> **Word Origins**
>
> **transmitted** The base word of *transmitted* is the verb *transmit*. It comes from the Latin word *transmittere*. *Trans-* means "across" and *-mittere* means "send."

transported (trăns•**pôr'**•tĭd) *v.* If something is transported, it is taken from one place to another. Most of the fruit we buy is transported from international farms to the United States by ships.

trench (trĕnch) *n.* A trench is a long, narrow groove or ditch. Heavy machinery is used to dig a long trench.

trickster (**trĭk'**•stər) *n.* A trickster is a character who deceives or tricks others, usually to get something from them. The fox is often portrayed as a crafty trickster in folktales.

U

unique (yoō•**nēk'**) *adj.* Something that is unique is different or one of a kind. Every snowflake is unique because it has its own special pattern.

V

vital (**vīt'**•l) *adj.* If something is vital, it is needed or very important. Water is vital to all living things.

vividly (**vĭv'**•ĭd•lē) *adv.* If you remember something vividly, you have a clear, detailed memory of it. As she wrote a story about her summer vacation, Nora vividly remembered her family's trip to the beach.

W

withered (**wĭth'**•ərd) *v.* If a plant has withered, it has dried up and died. The flowers hanging on the porch have withered.

wrath (răth) *n.* Wrath is strong anger. If you are filled with wrath, you might find it difficult to control your anger.

ă rat / ā pay / â care / ä father / ĕ pet / ē be / ĭ pit / ī pie / î fierce / ŏ pot / ō go / ô paw / ôr for / oi oil / oŏ book /

Index of Titles and Authors

Aesop, 112

Baik, Carol R., 46

Bug Bites, 170

Cooper's Lesson, 336

Dávila, Claudia, 204

Dawson, Nancy, 238

Dolphin Dinner, 330

Eco-Friendly Food, 152

Grand Canyon: A Trail Through Time, 56

Hayes, Joe, 100

History of Communication, The, 302

How Can We Reduce Household Waste?, 252

In the Days of King Adobe, 100

Johnson, Jen Cullerton, 272

Kennedy, X.J., 46

Kids Rock Nutrition in the Kitchen, 164

Kimmel, Eric A., 122

Levy, Oded, 138

Luz Sees the Light, 204

Mariana Trench, 16

Matthews, Caitlín, 112

Matthews, John, 112

Nature's Wonders: Poetry About Our Amazing Earth, 46

New Language—Invented by Kids!, A, 322

Nolen, Jerdine, 80

Now You're Cooking!, 180

On Sea Turtle Patrol, 238

Pair of Tricksters, A, 112

Pratt, Mary K., 252

Saldaña, Jr., René, 180

Saving the Kemp's Ridley Sea Turtle, 248

Sayre, April Pulley, 34

Schechter, Robert, 46

Seeds of Change, 272

Senker, Cath, 152

Shin, Sun Yung, 336

Simon, Charnan, 322

Ten Suns, 122

Ten Suns, The, 138

Thunder Rose, 80

Vieira, Linda, 56

Weird and Wondrous Rocks, 34

Withrow, Steven, 46

Woods, Mary B., 16

Woods, Michael, 16

Acknowledgments

"Aurora Borealis" by Steven Withrow from *Book of Nature Poetry* edited by J. Patrick Lewis. Text copyright © by Steven Withrow. Reprinted by permission of Steven Withrow.

"Bug Bites" from *ASK Magazine*, Nov. /Dec. 2004. Text copyright © 2004 by Carus Publishing Company. Reprinted by permission of Cricket Media. All Cricket Media material is copyrighted by Carus Publishing d/b/a Cricket Media, and/or various authors and illustrators. Any commercial use or distribution of material without permission is strictly prohibited. Please visit http://www.cricketmedia.com/info/licensing2 for licensing and http://www.cricketmedia.com for subscriptions.

Cooper's Lesson by Sun Yung Shin, illustrated by Kim Cogan. Text copyright © 2004 by Sun Yung Shing. Illustrations copyright © 2004 by Kim Cogan. Reprinted by permission of Children's Books Press, an imprint of Lee & Low Books Inc.

"Eco Friendly Food" (excerpted and retitled from *A Teen Guide to Being Eco in Your Community)* by Cath Senker. Text copyright © 2013 by Heinemann Library, an imprint of Capstone Global Library, LLC. Reprinted by permission of Capstone Press Publishers.

Grand Canyon: A Trail Through Time by Linda Vieira, illustrated by Christopher Canyon. Text copyright © 1997 by Linda Vieira. Illustrations copyright © 1997 by Christopher Canyon. Reprinted by permission of Bloomsbury Publishing LLC.

"The Great Barrier Reef" by Robert Schechter from the *Book of Nature Poetry*, edited by J. Patrick Lewis. Text copyright © by Robert Schechter. Published in 2015 by National Geographic Society. Reprinted by permission of Robert Schechter.

How Can We Reduce Household Waste? by Mary K. Pratt. Text copyright © 2016 by Lerner Publishing Group, Inc. Reprinted by permission of Lerner Publications Company, a division of Lerner Publishing Group, Inc.

"In the Days of King Adobe" from *Watch Out for Clever Women! Hispanic Folktales* as told by Joe Hayes, illustrated by Vicki Trego Hill. Text copyright © 1994 by Joe Hayes. Illustrations copyright © 1994 by Vicki Trego Hill. Reprinted by permission of Cinco Puntos Press.

"The History of Communication" (excerpted and titled from *Inventions and Discoveries: Communication)* published by World Book, Inc. Copyright © 2009 by World Book, Inc. Reprinted by permission of World Book, Inc.

Material from *Luz Sees the Light* written and illustrated by Claudia Dávila. Copyright © 2011 by Claudia Dávila. Reprinted by permission of Kids Can Press Ltd., Toronto, Canada.

"Mariana Trench" (excerpted and titled from *Seven Natural Wonders of the Arctic, Antarctica, and the Oceans*) by Michael Woods and Mary B. Woods. Text copyright © 2009 by Michael Woods and Mary B. Woods. Reprinted by permission of Twenty-First Century Books, a division of Lerner Publishing Group, Inc.

"The Mariana Trench" by X.J. Kennedy from the *National Geographic Book of Nature Poetry* edited by J. Patrick Lewis. Text copyright © 2015 by X.J. Kennedy. Reprinted by permission of X.J. Kennedy.

"A New Language--Invented by Kids!" by Charnan Simon from *ASK Magazine*, September 2010. Text copyright © 2010 by Carus Publishing Company. Reprinted by permission of Cricket Media. All Cricket Media material is copyrighted by Carus Publishing d/b/a Cricket Media, and/or various authors and illustrators. Any commercial use or distribution of material without permission is strictly prohibited. Please visit http://www.cricketmedia.com/info/licensing2 for licensing and http://www.cricketmedia.com for subscriptions.

"On Sea Turtle Patrol" by Nancy Dawson, illustrated by Denise Ortakales, from *Cricket Magazine*, May/June 2015. Text copyright © 2015 by Carus Publishing Company. Reprinted by permission of Cricket Media. All Cricket Media material is copyrighted by Carus Publishing d/b/a Cricket Media, and/or various authors and illustrators. Any commercial use or distribution of material without permission is strictly prohibited. Please visit http://www.cricketmedia.com/info/licensing2 for licensing and http://www.cricketmedia.com for subscriptions.

"A Pair of Tricksters" (retitled from "Raven and Crayfish") from *Trick of the Tale: A Collection of Trickster Tales* by John and Caitlin Matthews, illustrated by Tomislav Tomic. Text copyright © 2008 by John and

Caitlin Matthews. Illustrations copyright © 2008 by Tomislav Tomic. Reprinted by permission of Candlewick Press and Templar Publishing.

Excerpt from *Seeds of Change* by Jen Cullerton-Johnson, illustrated by Sonia Lynn Sadler. Text copyright © 2010 by Jen Cullerton Johnson. Illustrations copyright © 2010 by Sonia Lynn Sadler. Reprinted by permission of Lee & Low Books Inc.

Ten Suns: A Chinese Legend by Eric A. Kimmel, illustrated by YongSheng Xuan. Text copyright © 1998 by Eric A. Kimmel. Illustrations copyright © 1998 by YongSheng Xuan. Reprinted by permission of Eric A. Kimmel and YongSheng Xuan.

Thunder Rose by Jerdine Nolan, illustrated by Kadir Nelson. Text copyright © 2003 by Jerdine Nolan. Illustrations copyright © 2003 by Kadir Nelson. Reprinted by permission of Houghton Mifflin Harcourt Publishing Company.

Credits